SKYDANCE
ANIMATION
WONDLA
The Art & Making of the Limited Series

WondLa: The Art & Making of the Limited Series

ISBN: 9781835410424

Published by Titan Books
A division of Titan Publishing Group Ltd.
144 Southwark St.
London
SE1 0UP

FIRST EDITION: October 2025
10 9 8 7 6 5 4 3 2 1

EU RP (for authorities only)
eucomply OÜ Pärnu mnt 139b-14 11317
Talinn, Estonia
hello@eucompliancepartner.com
+3375690241

DID YOU ENJOY THIS BOOK?

We love to hear from our readers.
Please e-mail us at: readerfeedback@titanemail.com or write to Reader Feedback at the above address.

To receive advance information, news, competitions, and exclusive offers online, please sign up for the Titan newsletter on our website:
www.titanbooks.com

A CIP catalogue record for this title is available from the British Library.

SKYDANCE ANIMATION

WONDLA

The Art & Making of the Limited Series

RAMIN ZAHED

TITAN BOOKS

CONTENTS

FOREWORD

OPPOSITE PAGE
Artwork by
Nicolas Weis

MANY SCIENCE-FICTION STORIES WARN of a dystopian reality looming like an ominous thunder cloud that can't be avoided. A dark future rolls in and mankind is drenched in remorse for his folly.

This is not that story.

The books I enjoyed as a kid had their dark moments—as all good fairy tales do—but ended on a positive note. Perhaps not as simply as "happily ever after", but with a general feeling of optimism and hope.

The Search for WondLa sat inside me for over a decade as I figured out what this story was about. I was inspired by the birth of my daughter and my favorite childhood books like *Peter Pan & Wendy, Alice's Adventures in Wonderland* and *The Wonderful Wizard of OZ.*

Those stories focus on a girl protagonist who leaves the comfort and doldrums of home to escape into a wonderworld of fanciful characters. In the end, the heroine usually gains a better sense of herself, realizes the security found in family and longs for the safety of home. I wondered what would happen if I removed the reward of returning to one's refuge and instead had the heroine adapt to her new reality as home, and accept the characters that she'd traveled with as her new family. Because that is the future.

Our world is changing at a rapid rate. The reality my daughter faces when she is my age will be very different than the world I see before me now. I want her to adapt and flourish throughout these changes, love—and find love—where she can, while showing compassion for all living things. My hope is that her future, like Eva 9's, will have the sun shining down upon her long after the rainclouds drift away.

My newfound family at Skydance Animation felt the same, as you will see in this amazing collection of inspired artwork and design. Their talented team of artists and storytellers is comprised from the best in the business. The care and attention they gave to each character, prop and set came from a place of enthusiasm and excitement, just as it was for me when creating this story. I hope you enjoy the visual journey we took together while adapting my book to screen. Most of all, I hope you enjoy Orbona!

– TONY DITERLIZZI

A NOTE FROM SKYDANCE

I STARTED WORKING ON ADAPTING Tony DiTerlizzi's rich and imaginative book series *The Search for WondLa* into a TV series in 2019. I was immediately drawn to his remarkable characters, powerful narrative and charming illustrations. We were blessed with a wonderful, tireless team at our studio who worked hard to stay true to Tony's original vision, while bringing their own creative insights and ideas to each episode. I hope you will enjoy reading about how our talented artists, writers and technological wizards crafted a stunning CG-animated world that draws you in with its unusual flora and fauna. I believe we can all learn from Eva 9's journey and feel more empathy for all the living things on our planet during these challenging years. As Tony points out in *The Search for Wondla*, "No living thing is insignificant."

– JOHN LASSETER

THIS SPREAD
Early concept art

THE SEARCH FOR WONDLA BEGINS

OPPOSITE PAGE
Book cover by Natalia Falciglia

OPPOSITE PAGE
Page artwork by Simon Baek

WHEN TONY DITERLIZZI SAT DOWN to write the first volume of his wonderful fantasy/sci-fi series *The Search for WondLa* about 15 years ago, he was going through a reflective period in his life. He had already wrapped up his best-selling *The Spiderwick Chronicles* books, and was ready to dive into a futuristic world. "My daughter was born in 2007, and I was thinking back on my own life and thinking about how much the world had changed in 40 short years. I was wondering about what Earth would be like when she turned 40 herself," he recalls. "That thought was a compelling drive as I set out to create the characters and the world of *The Search for WondLa*."

It was John Lasseter's son, Bennett, who brought the books to his father's attention. "Ben had read the books, and we tried to set it up as a live-action series with another studio, but eventually, the project ended up at Skydance because we could create all the creatures and environments in animation and stay faithful to the book," says DiTerlizzi, who is also one of the show's executive producers. "I was very excited to see the world animated because I grew up on Disney movies and I've seen every Pixar movie on opening weekends. I'm an artist so I was very excited when Skydance came onboard to develop the book."

He adds, "Of course, it's always difficult to condense books as features, and here, we had the chance to stay true to the episodic nature of the books. I have had the experience of seeing my work adapted into live-action successfully in the past [*The Spiderwick Chronicles*] and 've always seen how other projects developed and fell apart in the interim, so by the time John came on board around four years ago, we rolled up our sleeves and got going."

For John Lasseter, the show's executive producer and head of Skydance Animation, bringing *WondLa* (the TV adaptation's shortened title) into animated life offered the great opportunity to collaborate with a living author. The project also provided the two-time Oscar winner and the director of acclaimed animated movies such as *Toy Story*, *Toy Story 2*, *A Bug's Life*, *Cars*, and *Cars 2* to produce a hugely ambitious animated TV series.

"When I first came to Skydance in 2019, plans were already in place to adapt Tony's books into a TV series," he recalls. "I had made many features and shorts before, but this was the first time I was working on a TV series. I was amazed at how much filmmaking and storytelling this project was going to involve! We ended up making seven and one-third hours, spread out over 20 episodes and three seasons to represent Tony's three books. It was made in four years, which is roughly around the same time it takes to make a 90-minute feature, and our budget was actually less

the WONDERFUL
WIZARD OF OZ
L. FRANK BAUM

than a feature! But we held the quality bar very high. We figured how to use an iterative story process, where you write the script, look at it, do revisions, then storyboard the script, cut it on reels, look at it, then make revisions. Of course, we don't do it as much as we do it for features, but we insisted on this process for both the script, storyboard, and reel process in order to polish the storytelling before we start layout and the filmmaking process."

Lasseter praises the team at Skydance for rallying behind this special iterative process even though it was quite challenging for an ambitious project of such length which features so many characters and locations. "They held fast to the important notion that the story was the most important thing," he says. "Our production designer Andy Harkness and his design team did such an unbelievable job. They aimed really high as they had to get a lot of the design work done before the story was even locked on the early episodes just to get things going."

Another exciting aspect of the process for Lasseter was Tony DiTerlizzi's noble reason for creating the book series. "He wanted to create something for his daughter that would prepare her for the world," says the producer. "You get raised in a family and your parents and teachers teach you as much as they can, but then you finish school and college and move out of the house, and then immediately life starts coming at you with things that your parents and teachers didn't quite prepare you for. And how you approach those things defines the person that you become. That's why Tony wrote this book which follows Eva 9's adventures in an alien world."

The creative lead knew that it was important for the audience and the show's main character to learn and understand the world at the same time. The heroine, Eva 9, is a brave young girl raised in an underground sanctuary by a robot named MUTHR (aka Multi-Utility Task Help Robot) who's forced to explore the exotic world beyond her home to find other humans. "That's the number one philosophy of our storytelling," explains Lasseter. "We are with Eva 9 from the very beginning and see this world through her eyes: We see at the end of the first episode after she gets thrust up onto the surface, and she realizes that nothing about this world resembles what she was taught: All the plants and creatures are alien. We wanted to have the rocks, the water, the clouds, the terrain feel like Earth, but everything else is alien. She has one singular goal and that's to find other humans, to get reunited with her family. That was the driving force of Tony's books and that's what inspired us to bring these books to the screen."

WondLa showrunner and executive producer Bobs Gannaway says he was also naturally drawn to the heart and message of DiTerlizzi's books. "Just like Tony, I have a daughter, and we know that we are sending our kids out into a world that is quite different from the ones we were sent out to," he explains. "I love how he took that idea and super-charged it with Eva 9 in the Sanctuary and having to leave it for an Earth that is not quite Earth."

Gannaway, whose many credits include *Lilo & Stitch: The Series*, *Mickey Mouse Clubhouse*, and *Monsters at Work*, says he welcomed the challenge to work on an episodic series. "Streaming allows us to have this hybrid form, which can tell a complex story through many episodes with a feature quality. There used to be a separation between TV and feature animation, but streaming and new technologies have blurred that line."

He gives credit to the crew at Skydance in Los Angeles and Icon Creative Studio in Vancouver which helped realize this massive project and elevate the

OPPOSITE PAGE Artwork by Simon Baek

ABOVE
Column design for Caeruleans in the palace at Solas by Marc Gabbana

quality of TV animation. "One of the great things about working at Skydance Animation is the fact that the head of the studio is a creative artist who's done every job he's asking you to do," notes Gannaway. "So it's inspiring to work with John because he pushes us to be our best, elevates the work, and pushes for quality. The good part is that he is challenging you to be the best you can be, and the bad part is that you can't get away with anything! There is no smoke and mirrors!"

Gannaway also brings up the unique challenges of adapting a work that is loved by millions of readers as a 20-part series. "Anytime you set out to adapt a beloved book property, you want to stay true to as much of the story as possible," he adds. "But structurally, we needed to make a show that keeps the viewer at the edge of their seats after each half hour. A book also allows you to hear the main character's thoughts—but we work in a visual medium, so we have to get those thoughts across through dialogue, music, and lighting."

According to producer Tony Cosanella (*Scoob!*, *Planes*) *WondLa* features 159 characters and 139 environments overall—a stunning achievement for this kind of project. "I was excited to be part of a project that pushes the envelope in different ways," he says. "We took a lot of inspiration from Tony DiTerlizzi's original illustrations, and he was with us throughout the process. There were certain new designs and characters that we felt would enhance the storytelling, so we took some liberties with Tony's blessings. It was all done in the spirit of elevating the story."

Cosanella says *WondLa* was unique in the way different departments worked simultaneously to come up with its many backgrounds and characters. "From a production standpoint, it was quite amazing to spend so many months designing and creating these worlds and knowing that we wouldn't have the chance to revisit them," he says. "Our amazing production designer Andy Harkness really embraced the idea of moving quickly and efficiently to explore different options. The key was to make sure everything still lived and belonged to Tony's world. Because of the speed of the production, we couldn't always wait for the story to be completely locked down, so we had to roll the dice. We had to just take some risks in figuring out if a location or character would play a big part in the story. So, overall, I think we did a really good job at running parallel disciplines despite the fact that it was an unconventional approach to production."

WondLa's supervising director Andrew Schmidt also praises the dedication of the team at Skydance that took on the monumental task of bringing DiTerlizzi's world to animated life. "We had this amazing group of people who were tested beyond their normal capabilities," he says, "and they all came through with flying colors. There was a lot of talking each other off the wall, but everyone just kept digging in and realized that we had something truly special. There was that Pixar and Lasseter ethos of everyone looking for ways to improve the work, and everyone kept improving it any way they could. That was truly remarkable."

Schmidt, who has worked as an animator on classics such as *The Iron Giant*, *Monsters, Inc.*, *Finding Nemo*, *The Incredibles*, *Toy Story 3* and *4*, *WALL-E*, and *Up* and directed Guillermo del Toro's *Tales of Arcadia*, says the character of Eva 9 will always stand out for him. "Our main character has this enthusiastic, positive outlook, part of which is a result of her growing up underground and learning about the world through books," says the director. "She is very empathetic and cares about what other people and creatures are feeling. I think that quality can be very appealing especially for our time where social media's influence on people can be so negative."

ABOVE
Column design for Arsians in the palace at Solas by Marc Gabbana

ABOVE
Column design for the House of Ojo in the palace at Solas by Marc Gabbana

Among the many appealing aspects of the project for Schmidt was the fact that many of the series' wild mix of characters and species are inspired by existing flora and fauna in our own world. "What you have to remember is that in the book, a virus changed the existing wildlife on the planet, so everything had a basis on things that already existed, like the air whales or the Otto being a giant tardigrade, or Besteel being a mix of species," says Schmidt. "That was amazing to be able to develop that kind of fantastic world based on the wildlife on our planet. Of course, it was great to have Tony DiTerlizzi right there to help us stay on track. When you go from a book to film, things will deviate, but you don't want to stray from the essence and meaning of the original material. He was always there to listen and share his ideas and thoughts and keep us within the boundaries of what he had intended to convey."

The show's visual effects supervisor Josh Herrig says research was considered a core value and production tool for *WondLa*. "We researched and redefined everything from art department assets to our shots pipeline and how we could even hope to complete a project of this scale," he points out. "Our production methodology and schedule had to be broken down from a typical feature and put back together in a manner that would suit the break-neck pace we needed for a series. We rebuilt our 3D scouting and art department collaboration and our lighting methodology with the goal of always placing cinematography, story, and performance at the forefront of our mission."

Herrig and his team did extensive research into the formation of the Rings of Orbona through the destruction of the moon and how they would appear in the sky at our various locations and lighting conditions. "The team brought in former NASA rocket scientists to walk us through some of the science and logic behind how the rings might form, and how Orbona would thrive and collapse through the different *WondLa* narratives," he recalls.

The largest logical challenge for the visual effects team was the fact that *WondLa* is set in a massive world. "A 'travel show' like this where we visit new worlds at all times of day meant that we needed to accommodate anything the writers room threw at us," explains Herrig. "We needed a massive number of sets and props, lighting setups for each of those sets at all times of day and a very well-considered plan for re-use of all of those sets and props for all three seasons. Of course, the goal is to allow the camera team to point the camera in any direction… however, with *WondLa* we approached it like a live-action set for speed and efficiency. We only built what we knew would be on screen and painstakingly planned where the camera frustum would be pointed, so we never built anything that wasn't going to be in shot. The effects department also had significant challenges in scale and budget. For example, we had to create the spiderfish races with full fluid simulations for above and below water but also within a series schedule."

Animation supervisor Yuriko Senoo (*Bolt*, *Tangled*, *Blush*, and *Luck*) says getting the characters' complex and multi-shaded emotions across proved to be some of the animation team's toughest assignments. "John [Lasseter] always told us that less is more, so we focused on the story and the message," she notes. "Something like an extra hand gesture would distract from the focus of a scene. We referred to Tony's book for inspiration, and [animator] Carlos Baena had a whole collection of live-action and animation clips that I looked at for reference. For example, we looked at Cate Blanchett in the movie *Heaven* for some of the emotional scenes or Walter Matthau in *Grumpy Old Men* for Rovender and Jason Bateman in *Ozark* for Cadmus. The recorded videos of actress Jeanine Mason who voices Eva 9 were also a huge help for us."

ABOVE
Column design for the House of Halcyonus in the palace at Solas by Marc Gabbana

OPPOSITE PAGE
Final render by Andy Harkness, Kuba Kozlowski, and Kalina Murat

Senoo also praises the nuanced depictions of both the main and the minor characters throughout the show. "You are never quite sure if a character is good or evil, until the very end," she says. "You are kept in suspense. Cadmus seems like a warm, fatherly figure, but then you discover that he has a dark plan. Even Eva 9's relationship with MUTHR and Eva 8 are very complicated. Nothing is black and white, and that makes the whole experience even more interesting and involved."

Series editor Torbin Bullock, an animation industry veteran who has worked on numerous Pixar films (from *Toy Story* all the way up to *Inside Out 2*), says he also enjoyed the subtle way *WondLa* manages to balance the personal moments with grand, epic set pieces. "The show is designed as a slow burn, and I'm so glad that Skydance convinced Apple to produce the entire project as three continuous seasons. As the series moves forward, it starts to really coalesce, and our production partners Icon in Canada rose to the challenge of taking on this massive job."

He adds, "One of the things I love about the show is that we managed to capture the intensity of Tony's books and how our main character becomes less naïve and more aware of the world around her with each episode and season. I hope our audience also discovers and embraces the message of the books: stepping away from the comfort of family life into the big world out there. In the tradition of some of the best young adult fiction, *WondLa* is about a brave young character who is finding agency over time and realizing that life is all about overcoming obstacles in order to discover what's true and what's not. We hope our audience also enjoys the highly entertaining and beautifully crafted world of Eva 9 as much as we did."

CHARACTER

EVA 9

OPPOSITE PAGE
Artwork by Juan Pablo López

RIGHT
Final render

BELOW
Artwork by Saira Vargas

BOTTOM RIGHT
Final still

BRAVE, RESILIENT AND UNIQUELY EMPATHETIC, Eva 9 (voiced by Jeanine Mason) is the heroine at the heart of the show and carries audiences along with her as she makes surprising discoveries throughout the 20 episodes of *WondLa*.

"Eva 9 was originally inspired by my own daughter, who turned 13 when I was writing the book," says DiTerlizzi. "We didn't want her to come across as a cipher who just shares information with the viewer. We wanted everyone to fall in love with her and we also wanted to show how quirky she was. It was exciting to be able to go back and think about how we portray her wonderful personality through her actions and what she says. Jeanine Mason took the character to another level and helped create this enduring protagonist. I think she's more of a surly teen in the books, but she has more pluck and personality in the series."

He also adds that the character's uncommon compassion and empathy towards not just the humans but also towards all the animals and the world really makes her stand out. "I was inspired by Dorothy from *The Wizard of Oz*, Wendy from *Peter Pan*, and of course Alice from *Alice's Adventures in Wonderland*," says the author. "Those stories are also about a heroine leaving the comfort of home and befriending others in a fantasy world and gaining insights along the way."

RIGHT
Artwork by Saira Vargas

BELOW
Artwork by Juan Pablo López

OPPOSITE PAGE
Artwork by Juan Pablo López

According to Lasseter, the creative team decided to portray Eva 9 a few years older in the show because 16 is the age kids often start to assert their independence. "We also wanted the character to be aspirational, so that both younger kids and older audiences would want to follow her adventures," he explains. "We also felt that she needed to fight and jump and climb like an Olympic athlete. We looked at professional rock climbers' physiques to design her body. She needed to have the strength and capability to do all those stunts. Eva is smart, kind, and sweet, but she's also a badass!"

Gannaway points out that Eva begins the show with hair that is very production friendly. "She starts out with a very tight braid, but it begins to get frayed as she travels to all the different worlds," he says. "We have this progressional model of her hair throughout the episodes, as it loosens up because she's not going to any beauty salons along the way! Her hair color also changes later in the third season. It's all about what is going to help the story best and help us track her growth."

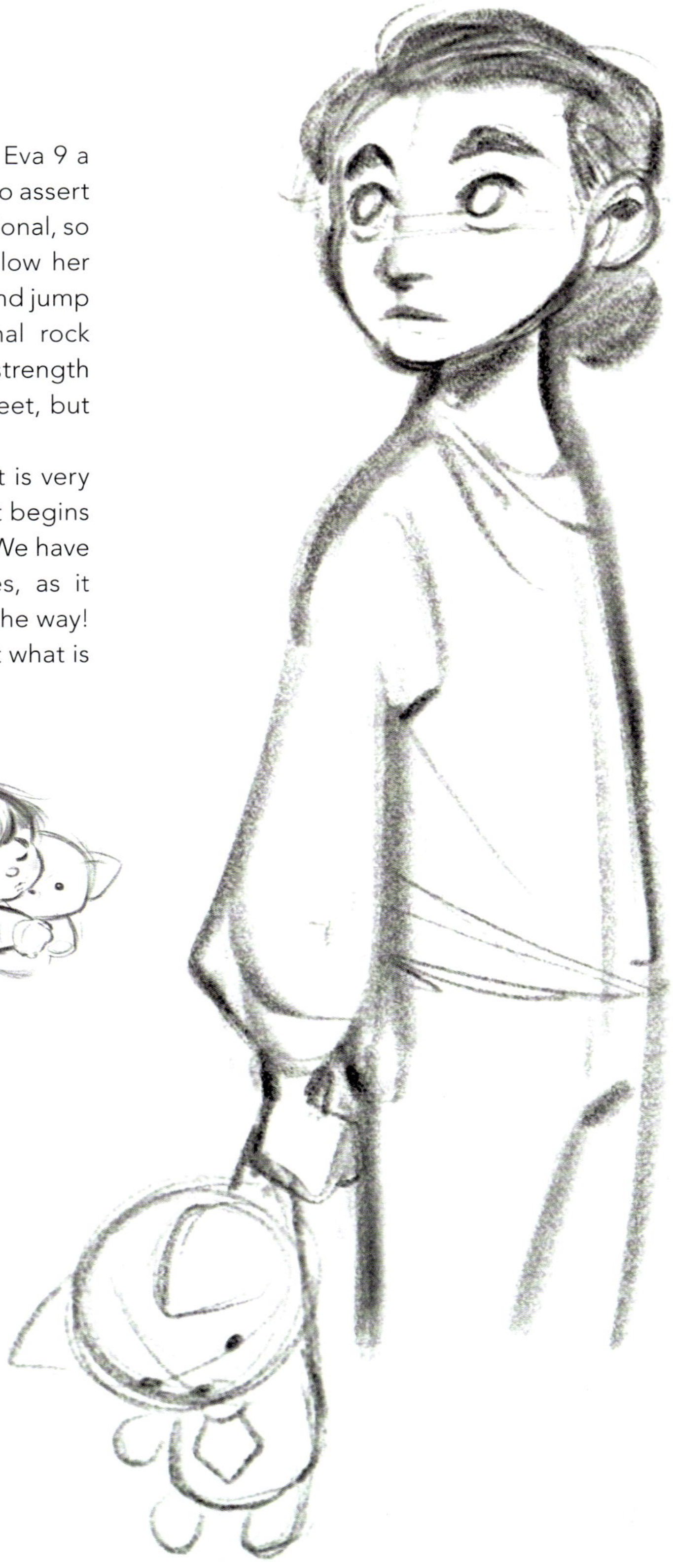

The task of designing the right outfits for Eva fell on visual development artist and costume designer Neysa Bove, a veteran of animated favorites such as *Frozen 2*, *Encanto*, and *Raya and the Last Dragon*. "We had to think about the type of costumes a character who grew up in a bunker would wear," she says. "These sanctuary children were trained to one day leave home and venture out to the surface and survive, so it made sense to think of utility tunics (clothing that you'd wear to survive different elements). This high-tech clothing needed to warm up or cool down the body, so I researched the outfits Olympic athletes wear for summer and winter sports. It would make sense that the in-show Dynastes brand would create a cohesive clothing line for the Sanctuary dwellers. So that's how we came up with what Eva and the other humans raised in the shelters wear throughout the series."

Bove also mentions that Eva's athletic shoes were specifically designed to have a tough sole so that they could weather any kind of terrain. "One big difference we added to her costume was a special spot for her Omnipod on her shirt," she says. "It kind of pops up in there and connects with the fabric. It was very utilitarian. Tony liked it too because it ended up looking a lot like an Apple product!"

LEFT & BELOW
Face study of Eva 9

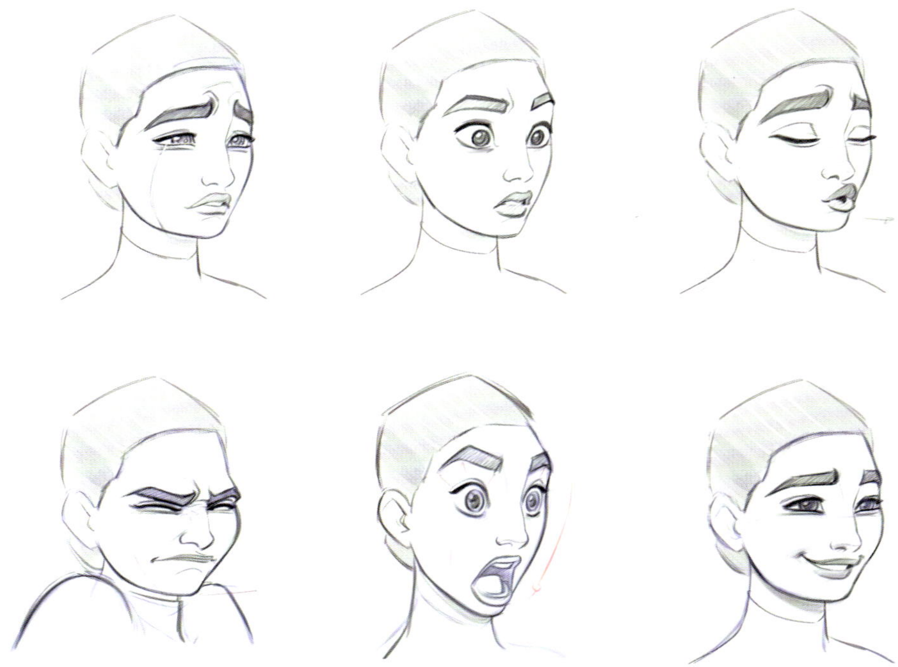

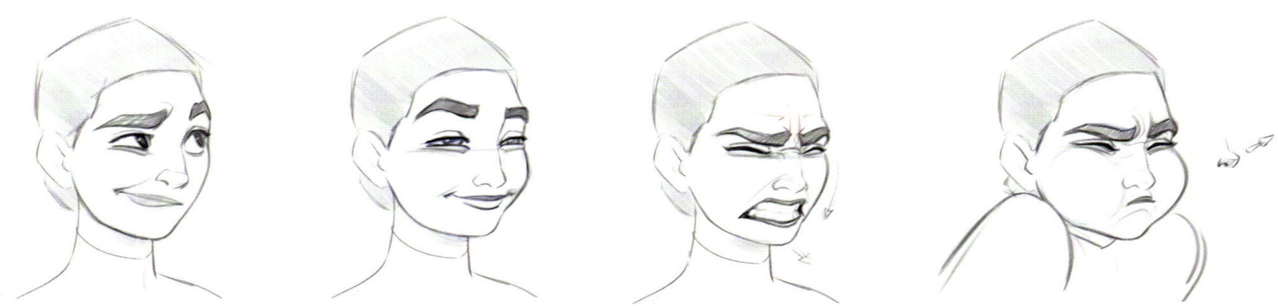

BELOW
3D render of Eva 9

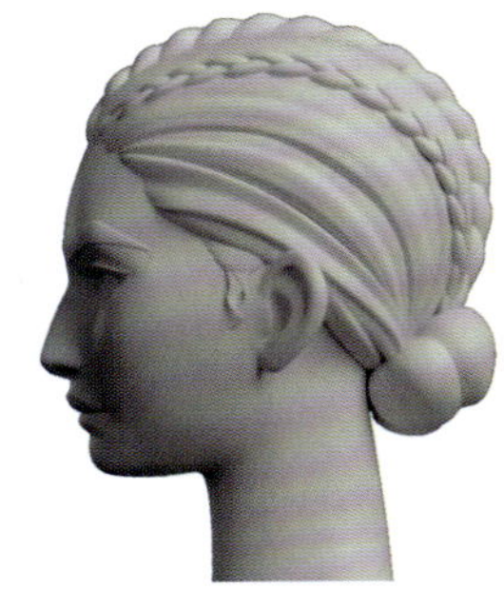

BELOW
Final renders of Eva 9 by Michele Graybeal

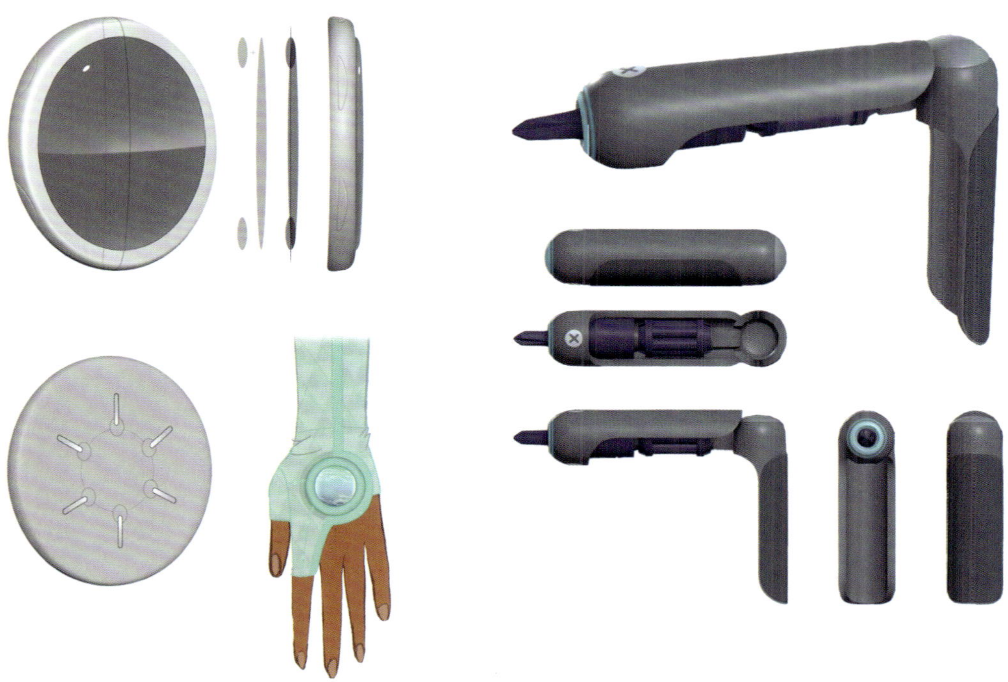

ABOVE
Costume designs by Maliheh Rahrovan

FAR RIGHT
Costume design by Neysa Bove

RIGHT
Omnipod and omnitool by Richard Lee

LEFT
Artwork by Sylvain Deboissey

ABOVE, RIGHT & BELOW
Artwork by Saira Vargas and Esther Wu

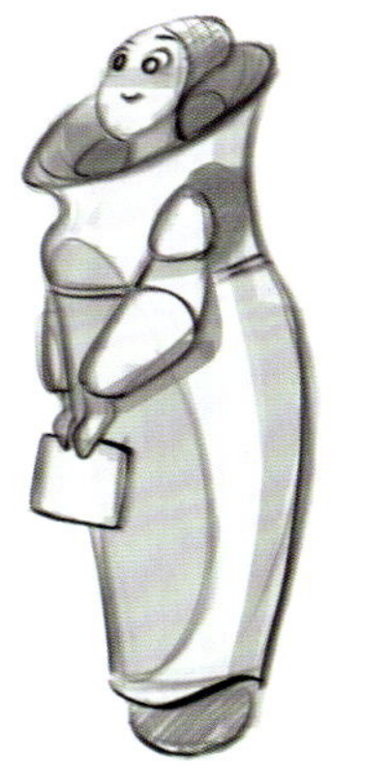

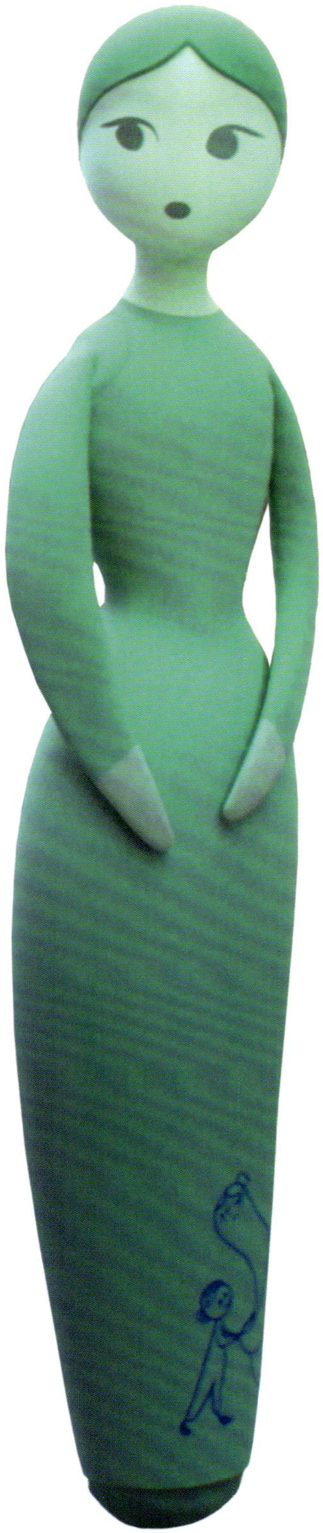

CHARACTER

MUTHR

MUTHR, AKA THE MULTI-UTILITY TASK HELP Robot 06, is the mechanical caretaker of Eva 9. She may be an AI unit, but thanks to the warm designs and voice-work delivered by actress Teri Hatcher, she cuts an unforgettable figure in the colorful realms of *WondLa*.

"MUTHR has a very retro design in Tony's books, but she looks quite different in the series," says John Lasseter. "We kept thinking about Steve Jobs and Jony Ive: what would they have come up with if they were designing this MUTHR robot? I remember Steve telling me that he didn't know one person who liked their cellphone and that he wanted to design a cellphone that everyone loved! For MUTHR, we wanted to do a similar thing and come up with a robot that was built to be beautiful, soft and caring with a very pleasant color. She was made to raise an infant. We studied how the baby mind develops and imprints on the face of human

LEFT
Final render

BELOW LEFT
Artwork
by Sylvain
Deboissey

BELOW
Paint artwork by
Kalina Murat

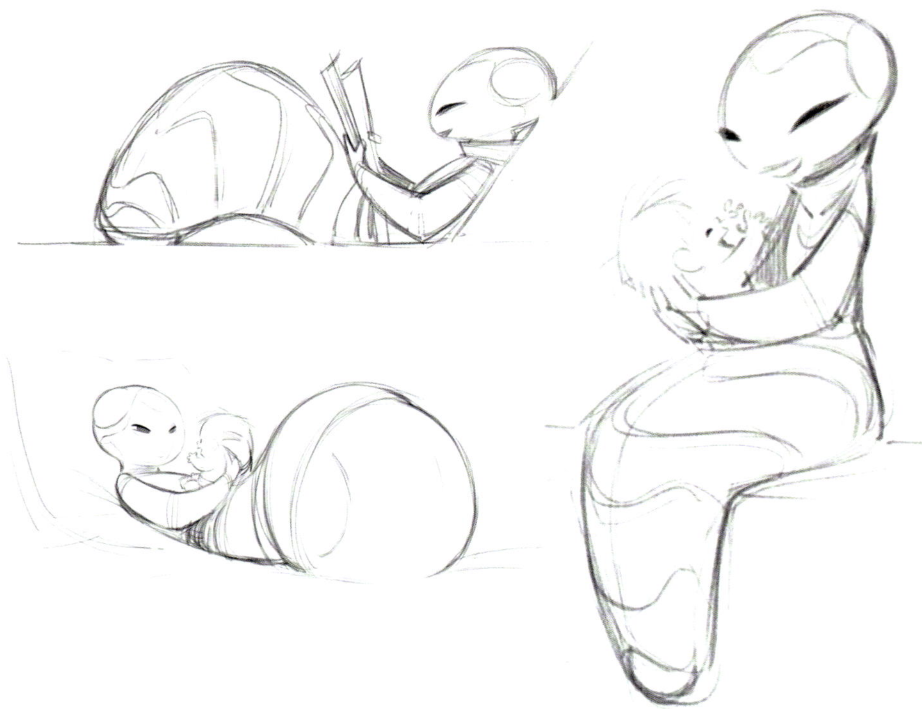

RIGHT
Artwork by Esther Wu

BELOW
Face study by Chris Ables

BOTTOM RIGHT
Render artwork by Richard Lee

beings. That's why MUTHR needed to have the eyes and the mouth of a human being. She needed to be appealing!"

The team found the perfect voice for MUTHR in Teri Hatcher, with whom Lasseter had worked with on the two animated *Planes* movies. "I knew she would be the perfect choice to voice MUTHR, as she had also narrated the three audio *WondLa* books. I said we must have her on the show, and Teri did a wonderful job bringing this character to life."

DiTerlizzi says his original designs for MUTHR were originally inspired by a series of ancient fertility figures from various prehistoric societies, so he sent those images to the design team for their visual update of the character.

"It was wonderful to have Tony DiTerlizzi along with us on the ride because he was a fantastic collaborator," says Gannaway. "With MUTHR, for example, we wanted to create a robot that looked new and different. She needed to be both maternal and cool. A lot of robots have a sort of mask in which the digital eyes and mouth live. We decided to get rid of that look and have her eyes and mouth be depicted with digital ink. Her surface also needed to both durable and soft, something you would have on a phone cover. Overall, I'm very proud of what we came up with in the final version, because she is futuristic, but also warm and appealing."

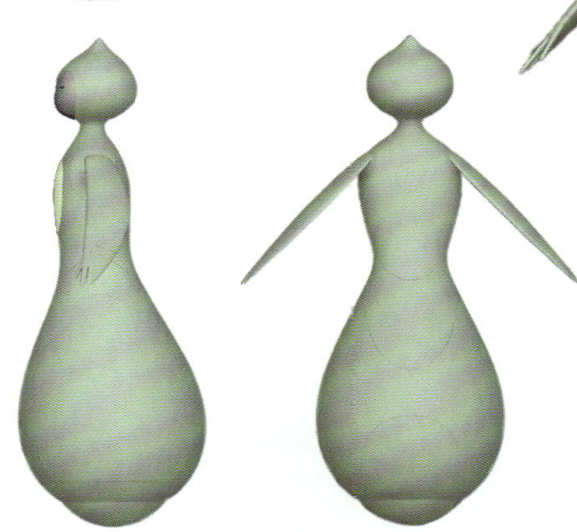
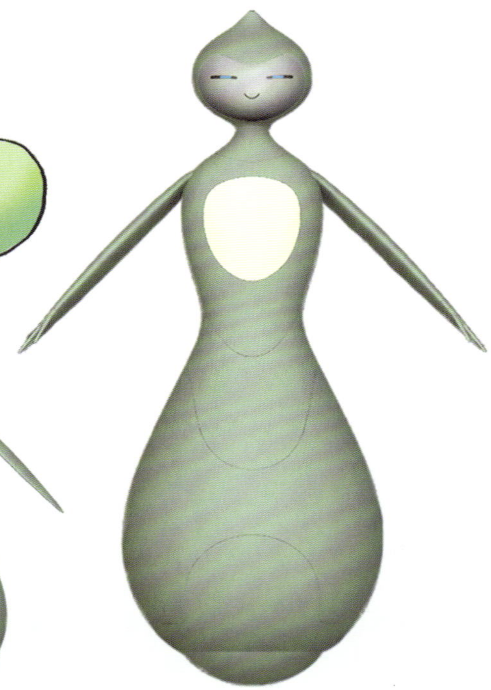

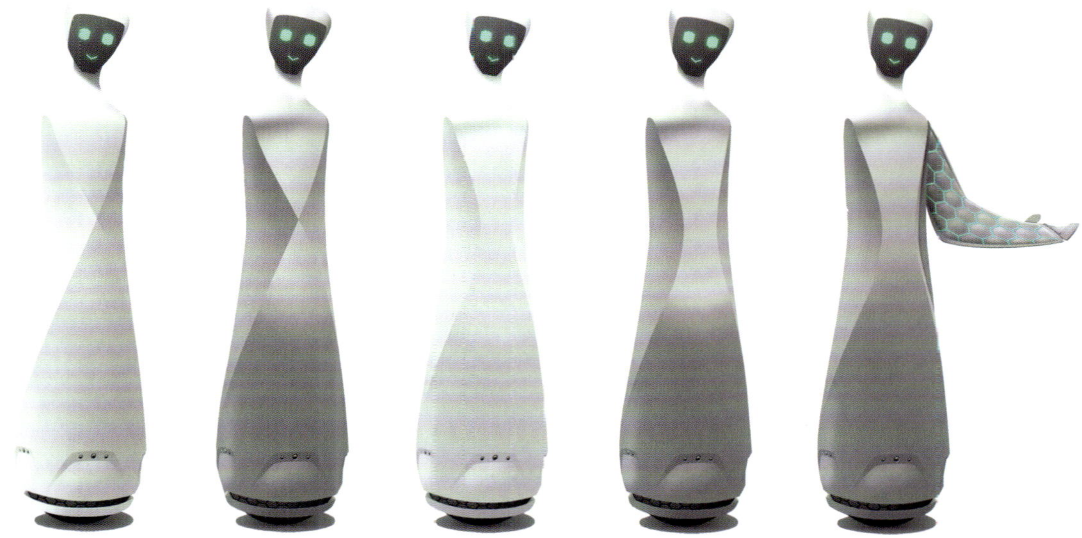

ABOVE
Artwork by Edwin Fong

TOP LEFT
Artwork by Saira Vargas

FAR LEFT
Artwork by Juan Pablo López

LEFT
Face study by Chris Ables

CHARACTER

ROVENDER KITT

RIGHT
Artwork by Sylvain Deboissey

BELOW
Final render

BELOW RIGHT
Artwork by Juan Pablo López

ROVENDER IS ONE OF THE FIRST ALIEN creatures Eva 9 encounters when she is forced to leave the comforts of the Sanctuary. Described in the book as a cerulean-blue creature with catfish whiskers who wears a faded brown jacket, large hat, and a rucksack, Rovender Kitt was designed to stand apart from the human dwellers of this world. Although he seems gruff and strange at first, he certainly grows on both Eva 9 and the audience with each episode.

"Rovender Kitt plays an important part in all three seasons of the show, so we needed his design to be appealing," says Lasseter. "Our design was fairly close to what Tony had in his books, but the audience needed to like him and get used to having him around just like Eva 9 does. We were also able to get a lot of humor out of his character, and Gary Anthony Williams did an amazing job of depicting his complicated

personality. Rovender has a difficult time letting Eva in at first, and we don't know why, but as the plot unfolds, we discover that he is hurting deeply because of the family he lost."

According to DiTerlizzi, Rovender Kitt was inspired in part by Rooster Cogburn, the gruff character played by John Wayne and Jeff Bridges in the two different adaptations of *True Grit* in 1975 and 2010. "He is the alcoholic, surrogate father who takes in the young, headstrong girl," says the author and executive producer. "He was such a fun character to write, and I thought it was pretty awesome that everyone was onboard to keep him intact."

Bove says that although Rovender was supposed to be gruff and rough around the edges initially, we needed to be reminded of the happier days he had spent with his family and his people. "We put more colorful patterns underneath his robe, and later on, he adds more and more layers on his tunic," she says. "There's also the sash he wears around it, which was part of his daughter's clothing."

Much of the iconography on the character's outfit is inspired by fossils. "When I talked to Tony about it, he showed me all these illustrations of microscopic creatures and remnants, and you can see their organic influence on the costumes as well," notes Bove. "John [Lasseter] also had this great idea to add some small shells on top of the robe's shoulders

TOP LEFT
Artwork by Juan Pablo López

ABOVE, BELOW & BOTTOM LEFT
Artwork by Shane Prigmore

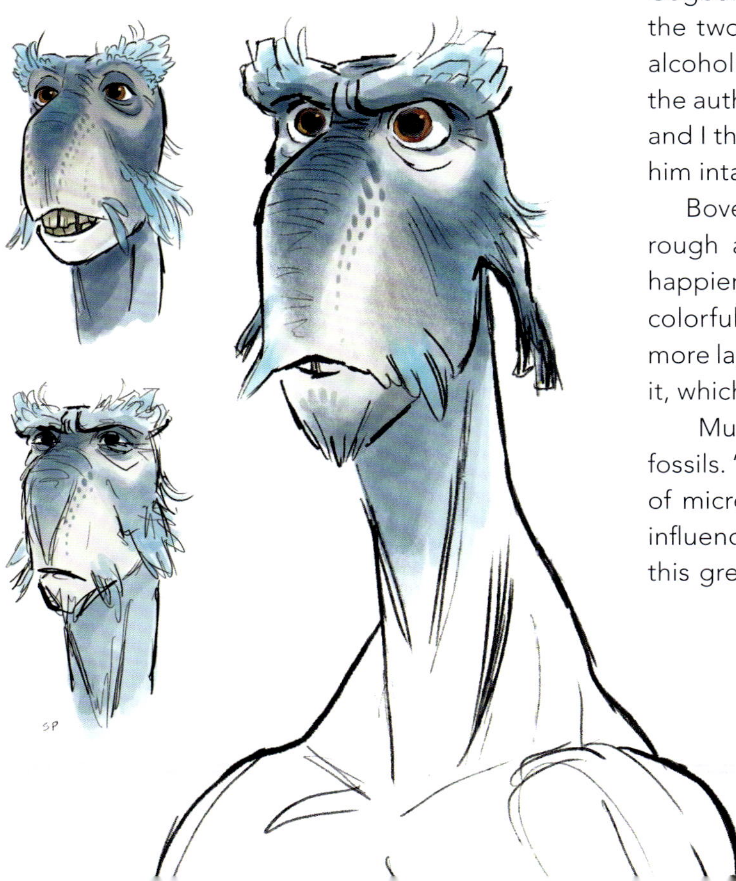

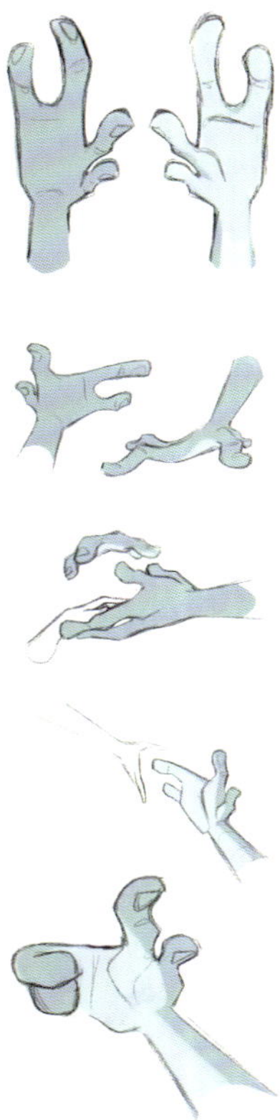

area, so that also added backstory to his outfit. His past is also reflected in the bandage he wears on his foot. It shows that he has seen some rough years, living out in the wilderness and just trying to survive. That is in sharp contrast with how Eva looks in the beginning of her journey as her machine-made clothes and hair are perfect. For Rovender and the rest of the Halcyonus residents, you want to feel that everything is handmade and asymmetrical."

Translating Kitt's unusual design to animation proved to be quite a task for the team. "Rovender was probably one of the most difficult characters to animate because his knees are backwards," Senoo remembers. "That was a tough one especially when he kneels downs. We had to cheat a little bit, and instead of the knees, we used other parts of his anatomy when he kneels!"

ABOVE
Hand exploration by Saira Vargas

RIGHT
Costume artwork by Neysa Bove

OPPOSITE PAGE
Paint artwork of Rovender Kitt's face by Michele Graybeal

FAR LEFT
Artwork by Shane Prigmore

LEFT
Pack, knife, and drinking gourd by Julie Chon

BELOW
Hat and walking stick by Christine Kim

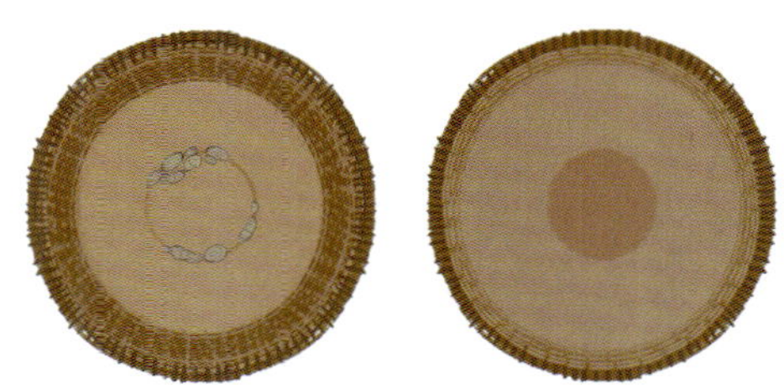

CHARACTER

OTTO

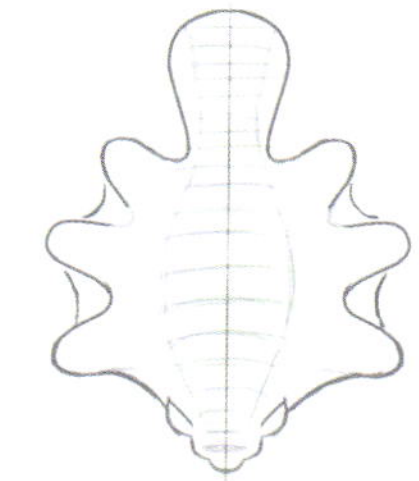

IT'S HARD TO BELIEVE THAT THE GIANT LOVABLE Otto (voiced by Brad Garrett), which acts like an eager-to-please family pet and carries Eva 9 and her friends through some treacherous terrain in the series is really an oversized tardigrade, or water bear (an eight-legged microscopic real-life animal) as identified by Eva 9's Ominpod. After our heroine rescues him from a trap early on in her adventures, Otto promises to look after her and be her faithful companion and guardian.

"Otto's name is an anagram of Dorothy's dog Toto from *The Wizard of Oz*," reveals Tony DiTerlizzi. "He is the family dog that Eva 9 always dreamed of having. He is like this wonderful, gigantic lovable dog that you just want to lay on and be with and cuddle with, but he's also very helpful to Eva 9, and she can communicate with him telepathically."

OPPOSITE PAGE
Artwork by Shane Prigmore

THIS PAGE
Paint artwork by Michele Graybeal

BOTTOM LEFT
Final render

THIS SPREAD
Artwork by
Martin Bergquist

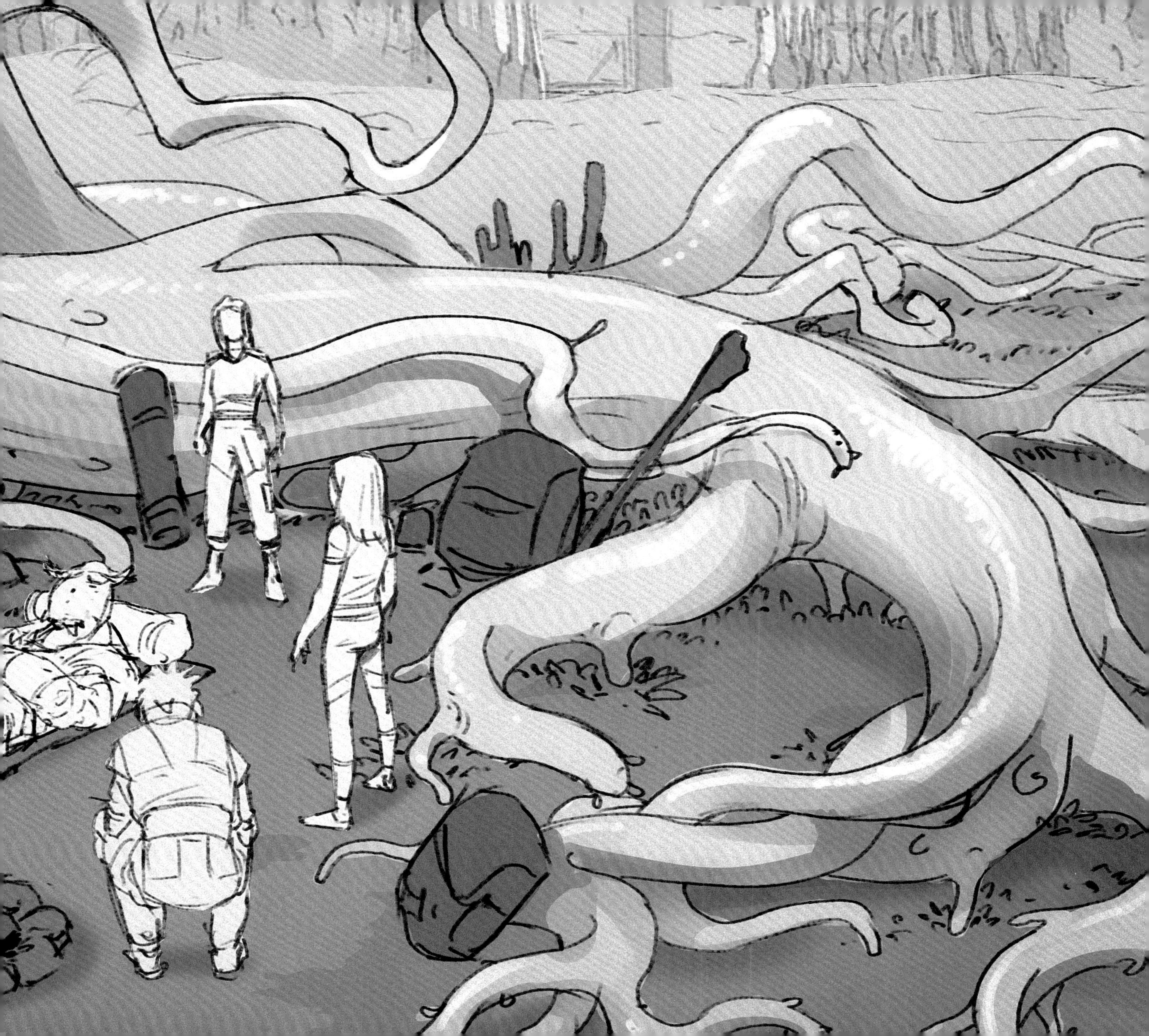

CHARACTER

BESTEEL

THIS SPREAD
Sketches by Sylvain Deboissey

THIS SPREAD
Paint artwork by Michele Graybeal

THE MAIN ANTAGONIST OF THE FIRST SEASON OF the show is Besteel (voiced by Chiké Okonkwo), a frightening beast and a Dorcean bounty hunter who works for Queen Ojo of Solas. Besteel damages the Sanctuary and MUTHR, and he continues to pursue Eva 9 and her friends relentlessly. His piercing yellow eyes and sharp teeth remind one of a predatory T-Rex. He has grayish black fur and several pairs of legs with talons. His two front legs double as arms, and he has two unused secondary arms beneath his chin. He is extremely skilled at using his powerful weapon called the Sonic Boomrod.

DiTerlizzi says Besteel was always meant to be very feral-looking. "I looked at predatory dinosaurs, owls, and orcas," he recalls. "His dappled camouflage was actually inspired by baby tapirs who have the same kind of rounded patches."

"Besteel may come off as a fairly stock villain in the beginning, but we later find out why he was so persistent," says DiTerlizzi. "I had all that information mapped out from the beginning, and I wanted to parse it out at the right time so that the reader and the viewer would discover the revelation in the second book and series, respectively. The best antagonists are the ones who have a reason behind their actions. We find out later that the reason behind Besteel's actions have to do with his brother and what he has done to prove his worth. It's all complicated because the story has always been about family and its complications. You will see that theme reflected in the backstories of many of *WondLa*'s characters."

RIGHT
Trap by JJ Song

RIGHT & BOTTOM RIGHT
Cage by Julie Chon

BELOW
Armour by Christine Kim

BOTTOM
Final render

Gannaway says he and his team were careful not to color him as a one-note character. "He's the monster in the house from the first episode, so I thought we always needed to define him beyond this terrible bounty hunter," he says. "You will find this in the small details we were able to include. There's a scene where Besteel is eating his barbecued meat, and he's just about to take a bite. Then, he decides to pull out some salt or spices and add it to the meat. I know it's not a big deal, but nothing is random in animation. The whole point of the scene was that even though he's a monster and he's shooting everything up, he still wants to salt his food. There's a hint of civility in his character. Sometimes, characters are defined by their big actions and big pieces of dialogue, and other times, you learn more from smaller gestures as you get deeper into their world."

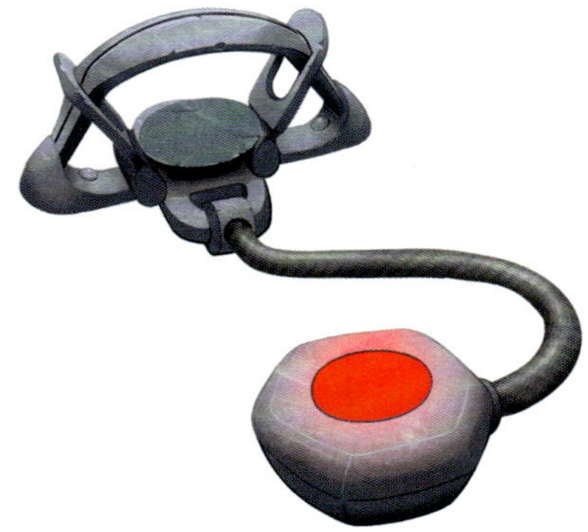

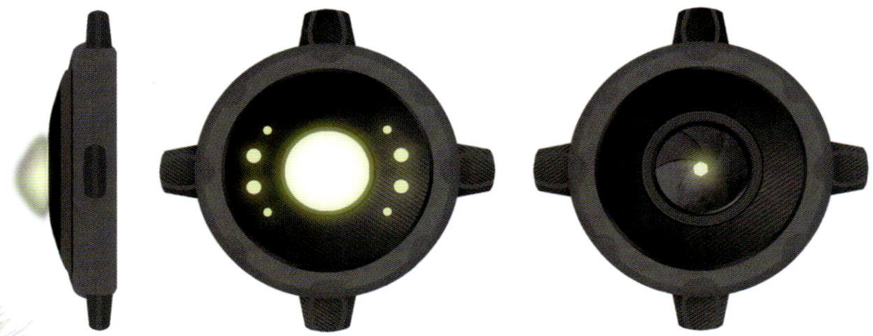

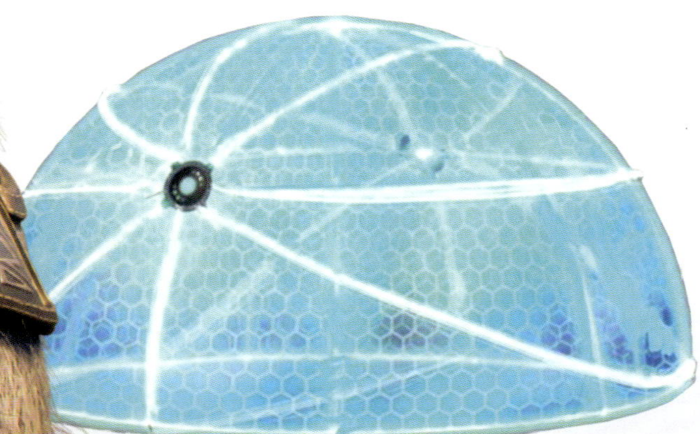

ABOVE
Boomrod by
Simon Baek

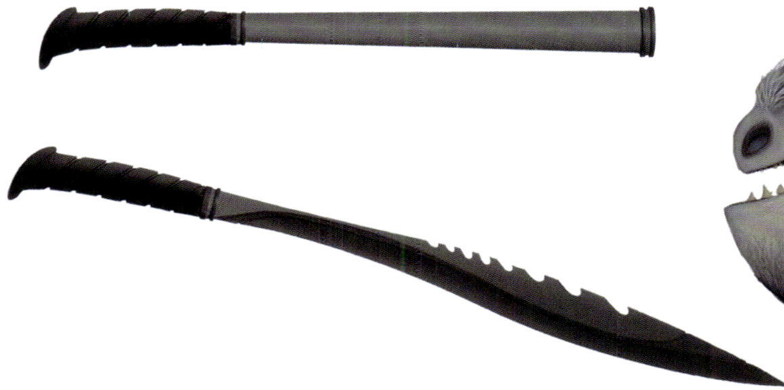

RIGHT
Weapons by
Julie Chon

FAR RIGHT
Paint artwork by
Michele Graybeal

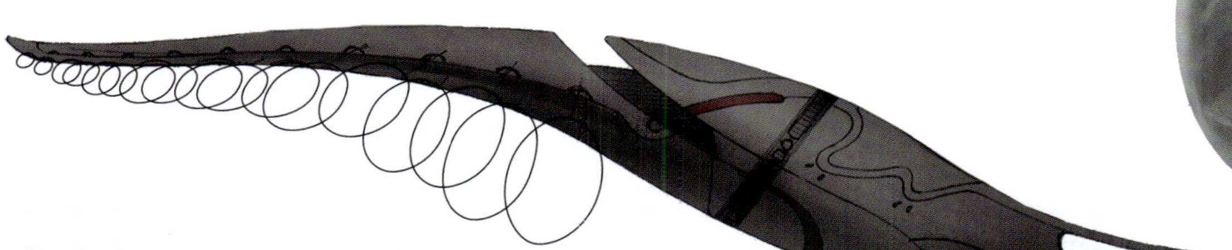

RIGHT & BELOW
Glider by Marc
Gabbana and
Simon Baek

CADMUS

OPPOSITE PAGE
Face study by Juan Pablo López

RIGHT
Costume design by Neysa Bove

BELOW RIGHT
Glove by Chris Ables

BELOW
Paint artwork by Michele Graybeal

CADMUS PRYDE IS THE LEADER OF THE UTOPIAN society known as New Attica, and he is also the brains behind the creation of Dynastes Corporation's Sanctuaries to protect human babies from the conditions on the planet. Like many of the characters in the book and the series, he is a complex figure whose plans and motivations are never as simple as they seem. He first appears to a younger version of Eva 9 in Episode 1 as a hologram, but he plays an increasingly important and complicated role as the show progresses. His role in *WondLa* and interest in Eva 9 are made clearer in the second season of the show.

Sporting a perfectly groomed silver mane and perfectly groomed facial hair, Cadmus is seen wearing comfortable long hunter-green or grey robes and a future-world take on Silicon Valley "tech bro" casual wear. He is voiced impeccably by much-loved and versatile animation world actor Alan Tudyk.

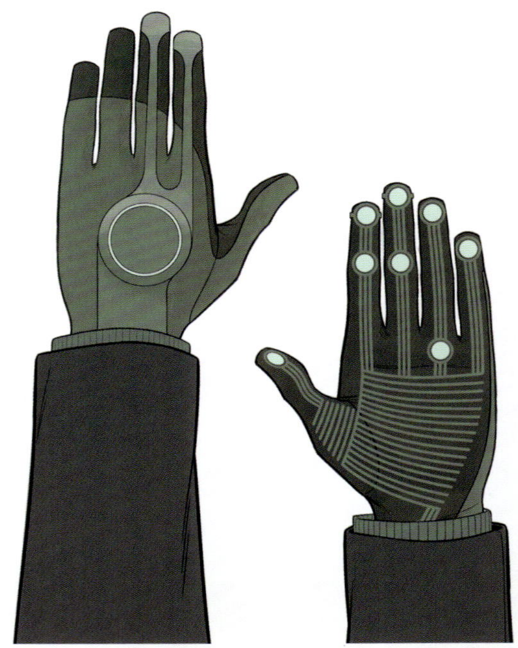

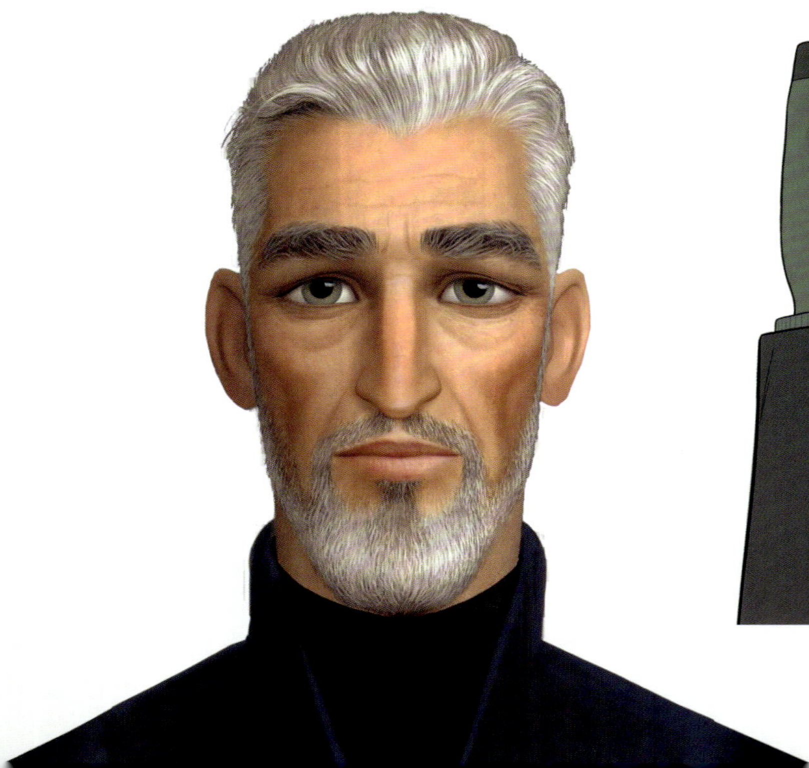

THIS PAGE
Artwork by Juan Pablo López

OPPOSITE PAGE: LEFT
Expressions by Chris Ables

OPPOSITE PAGE: RIGHT
Paint artwork by Michele Graybeal

573

LOCATION

SANCTUARY

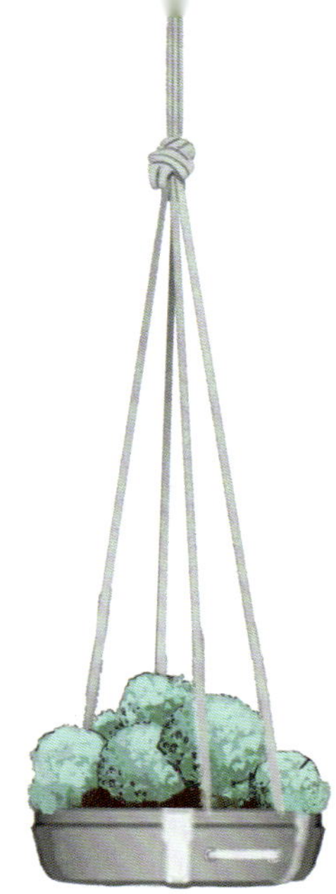

EVA 9'S JOURNEY IN THE BOOK AND THE SERIES begins in the technologically advanced Sanctuary built by the Dynastes Corporation. It was conceived by Cadmus Pryde to repopulate the Earth with humans. Each unit is equipped with a bedroom, kitchen, holography chamber, gym, greenhouse, supply and generator room, and is overseen by MUTHR.

DiTerlizzi says the idea for the Sanctuary came to him as he was thinking a lot about the end of the world and human civilization around the time he was preparing the book. "The premise that I had in mind was what if the technology we have is advanced, but not advanced enough to move the entire world population to another planet like Mars!" he recalls. "There's a section in the book about how they tried to colonize the moon, and it backfired, so in the series they show part of the moon is fractured to reflect that part. So instead, everyone had to go underground. At the time, everyone was also thinking about bomb shelters and bunkers. So, the thought was what if a big technological entity like Apple had designed this state-of-the-art sanctuary, and some tech giant was in charge of

OPPOSITE PAGE
Artwork by Marc Gabbana and Simon Baek

ABOVE
Plants by Kalina Murat

BELOW
Artwork by Kalina Murat

THIS SPREAD
Artwork by
Marc Gabbana

creating these fully automated bunkers that could grow test tube babies to repopulate the surface."

That idea led to similar ones about how to keep the humans' circadian cycles flowing smoothly, as well as their food supply, exercise, and education. "I started making notes about this weird futuristic hamster cage that the humans would live in," says DiTerlizzi. "I remember the designs all had rounded off corners, because you didn't want to have any sharp corners. "This would be an experiment so all foreign particles would need to be jettisoned, which is horrible but that's the price you must pay for survival and the reseeding of humans on the planet. The look had to be minimalistic, antiseptic, and sterile. Our design team did a terrific job of realizing it for the show, and you can really feel the Sanctuary's contrast with the rich world of the Wandering Forest outside."

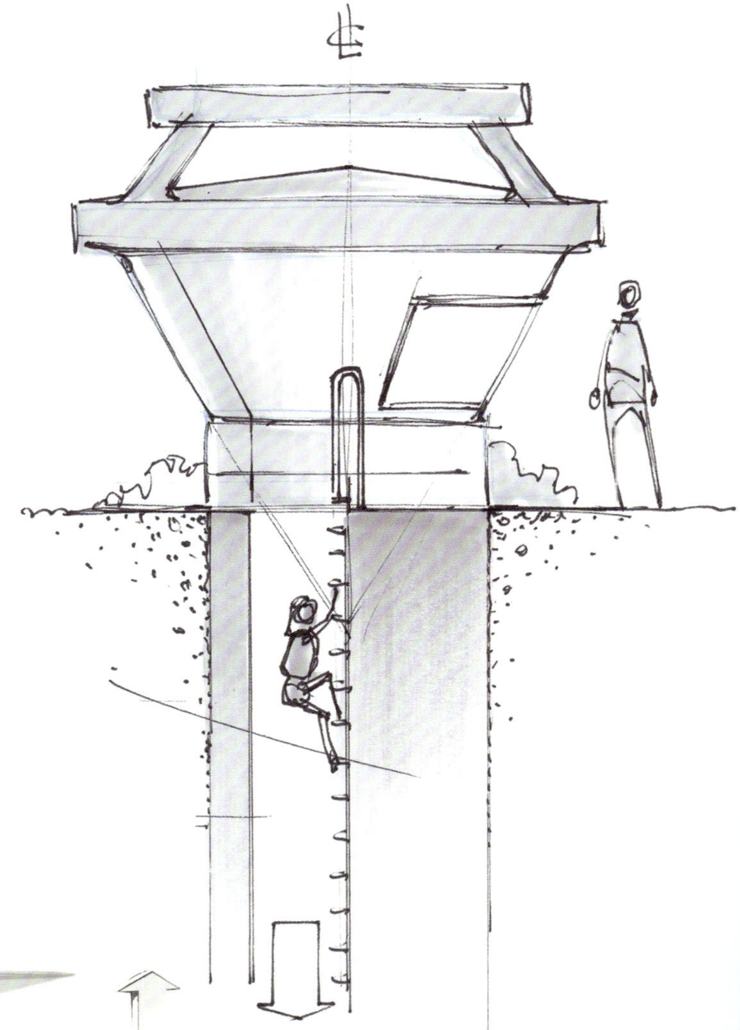

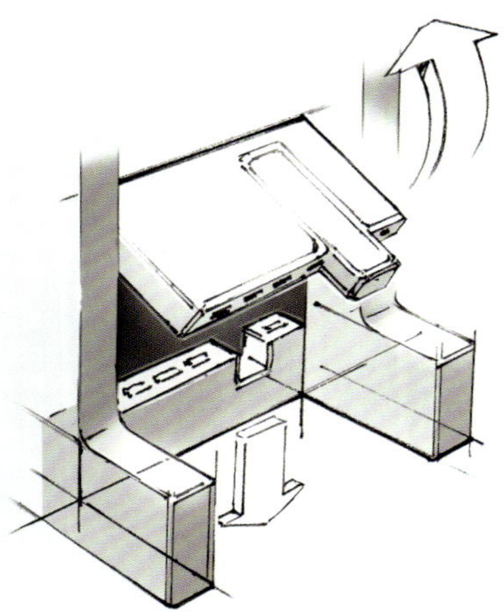

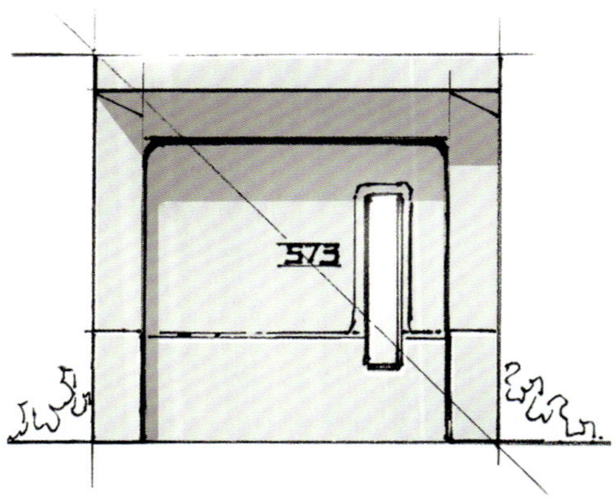

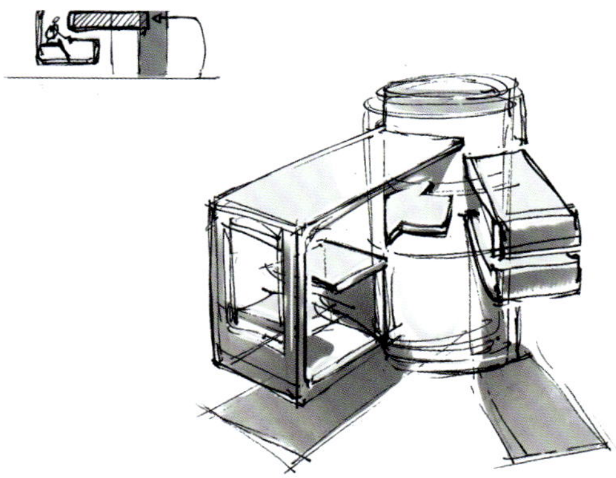

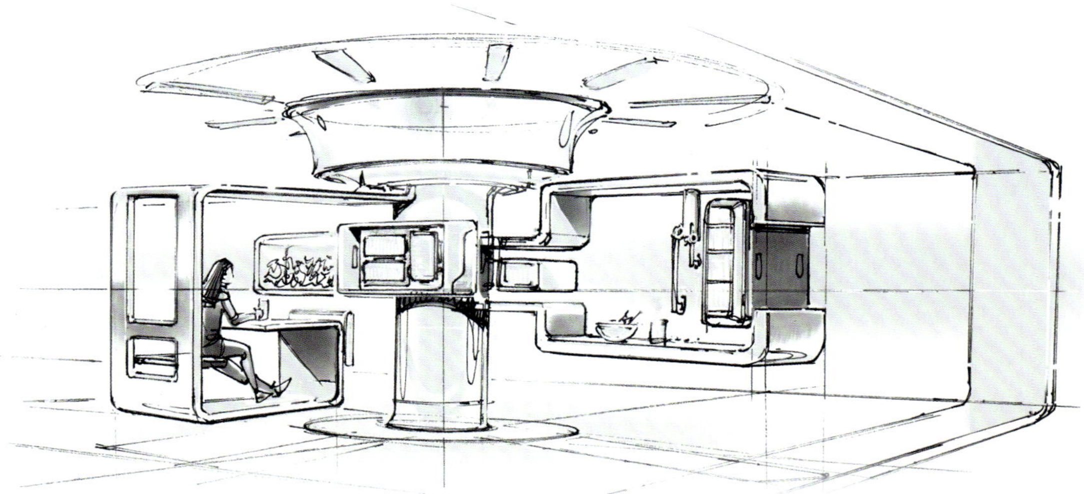

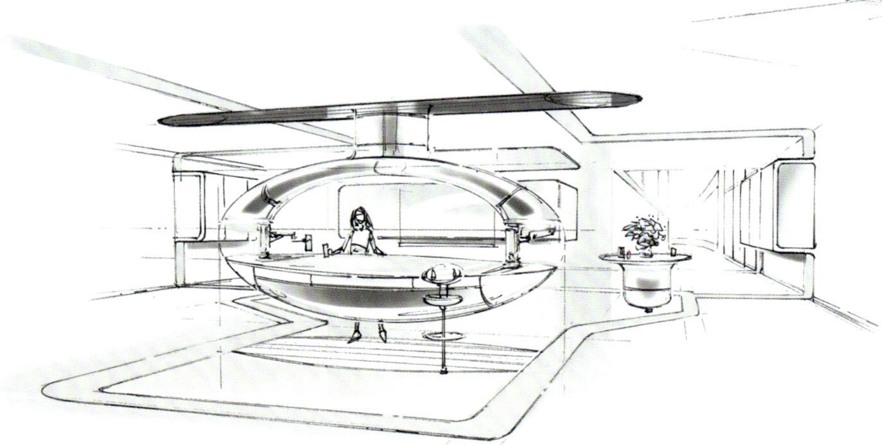

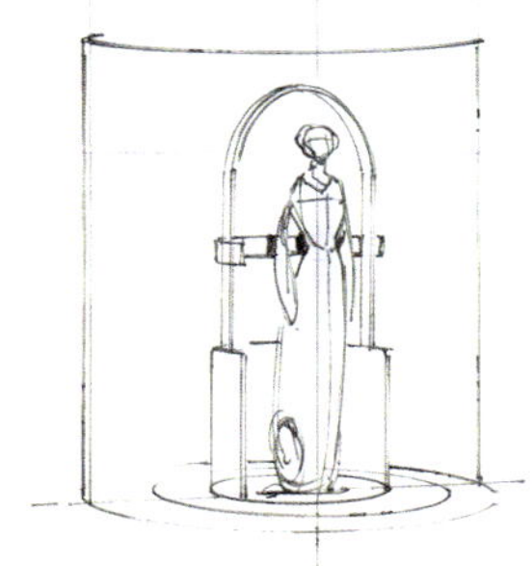

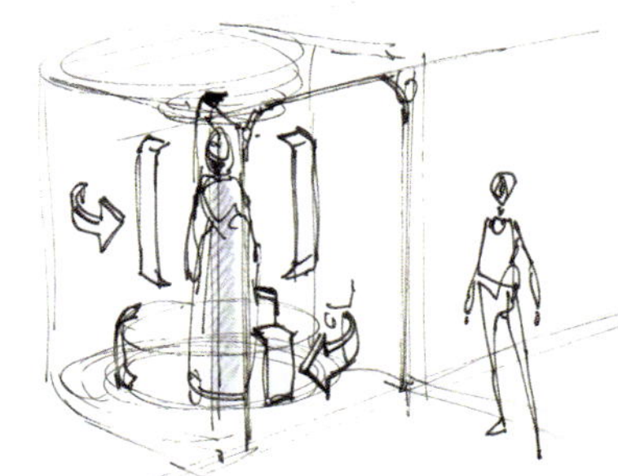

Harkness and his team followed D Terlizzi's cues. "We did massive research dives into everything that was high-tech related," he notes. "The color palettes had to be minimal. Everything had to be symmetrical with cut lines. We wanted to contrast the world of the Sanctuary with the asymmetrical wild world on the surface. It's interesting because Tony also has a little bit of a color shift between all three books of the series. In the first book, the colors were complementary, and you had many colors in the illustrations. Then, in the second book, we have a lot of blue washes, while the third book was warm with yellow and red ochre colors. Eva is almost overwhelmed when she comes up to the surface. We wanted viewers to feel the same way, because they've had one episode to get used to the simplistic colors, and then they'll be blown away by the outside world awaiting our lead character."

LEFT
Sustibar artwork by Craig Foster

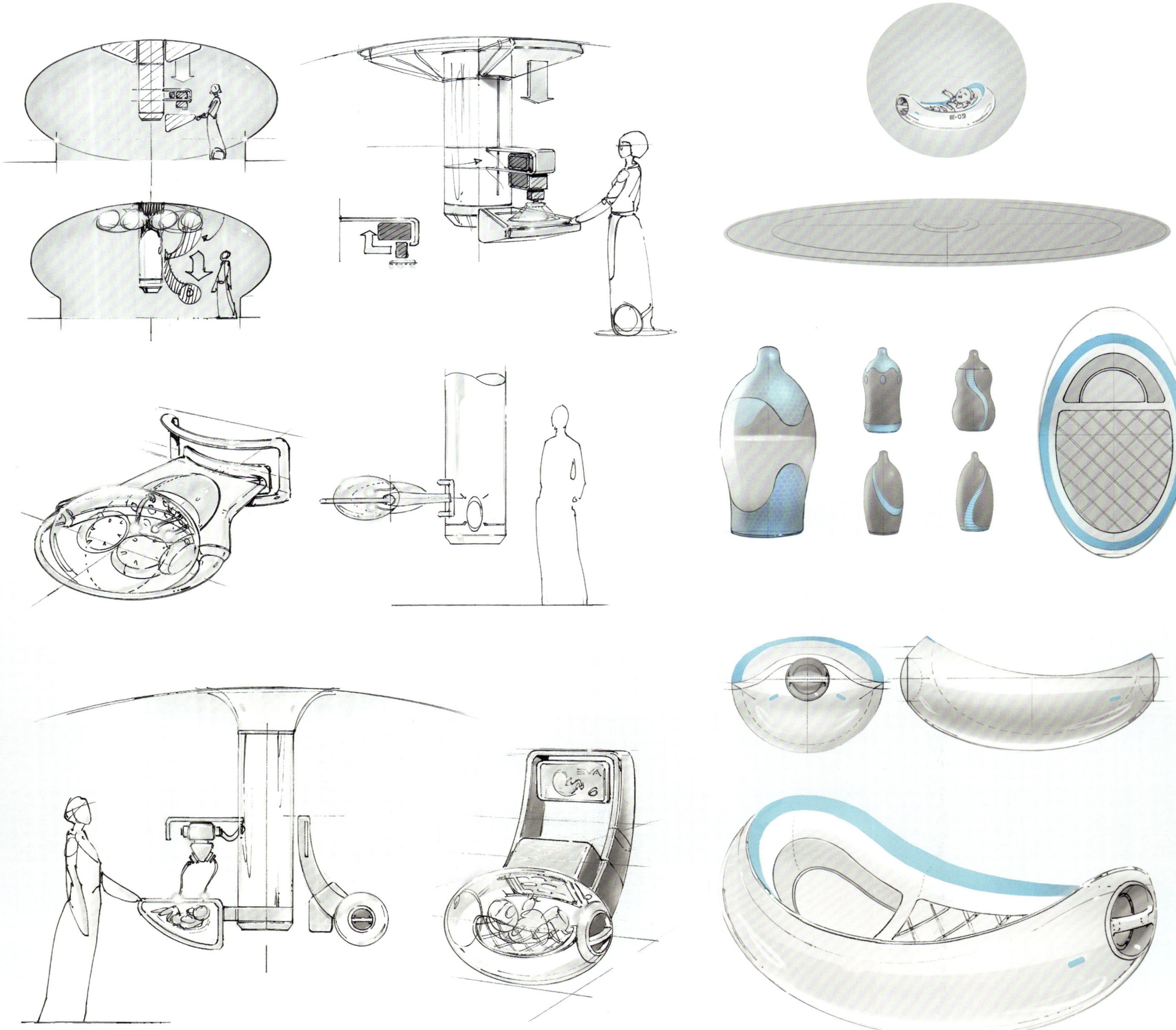

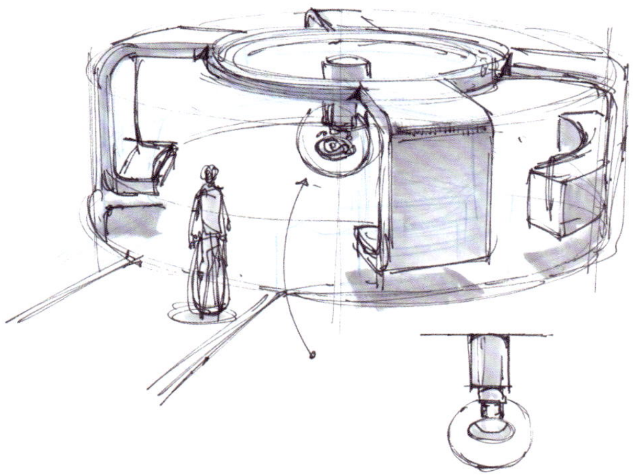

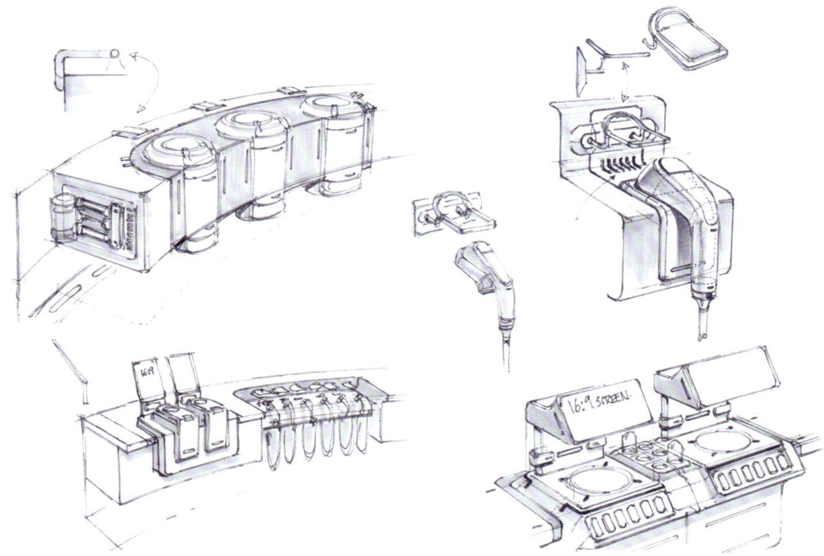

THIS SPREAD
Artwork by
Marc Gabbana

BELOW
Plants and
medical room
by Kalina Murat

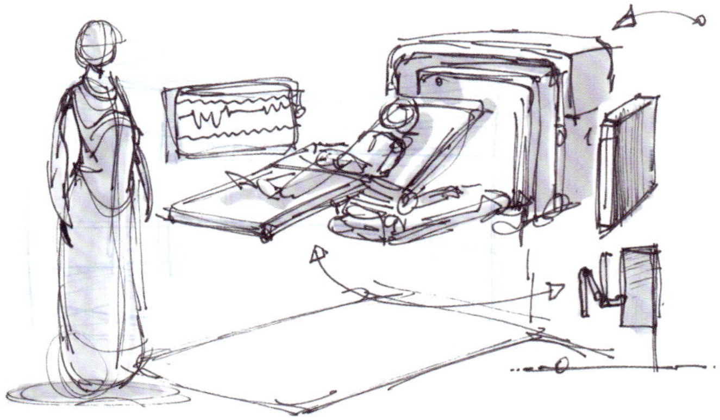

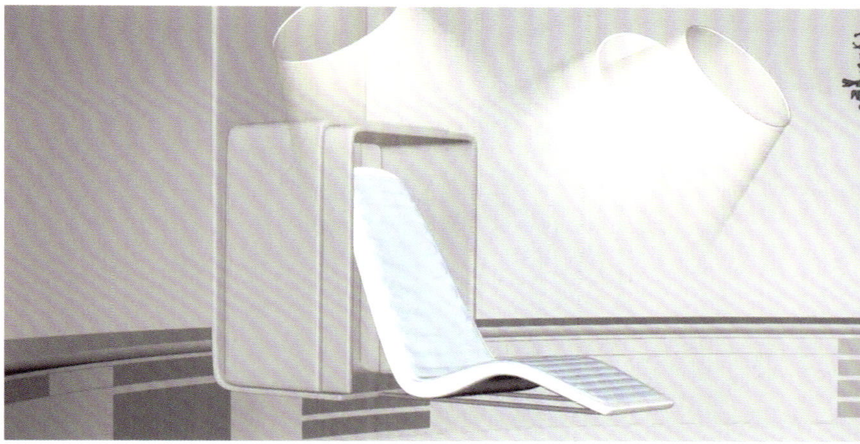

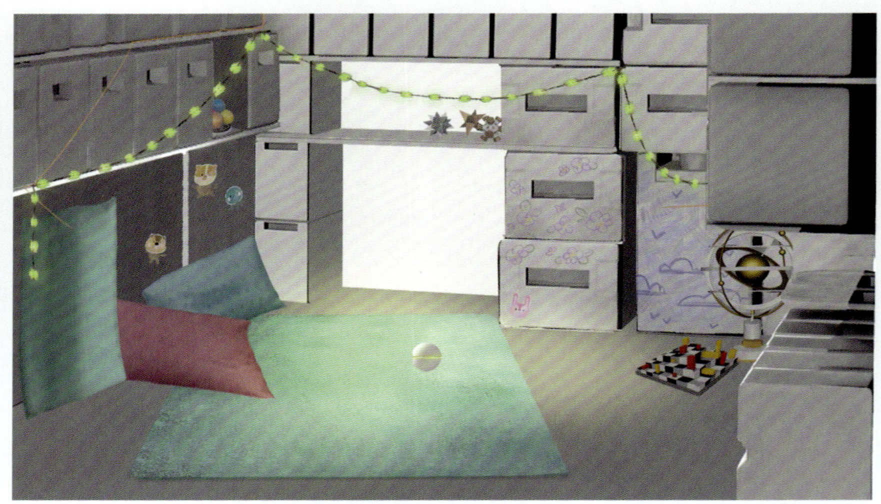

ABOVE
Artwork by Marc Gabbana

RIGHT
Store room fort by Kalina Murat

ABOVE RIGHT
Dynastes graphics by Craig Foster

OPPOSITE PAGE
Artwork by Marc Gabbana and Simon Baek

LOCATION

ORBONA

OPPOSITE PAGE
Concept art

ACCORDING TO THE *WONDLA* BOOK TRILOGY, Orbona is actually Earth, many years after humans destroyed the biosphere and life on the planet. It's now inhabited by various alien races such as Arsians, Caeruleans, Halcyonus, and Dorceans who brought life back to the planet by using the Vitae virus, a biochemical agent that interacts with existing organisms and causes them to mutate and increase in size. The Sanctuary, Lacus, Solas, and the Wandering Forest are all part of Orbona.

DiTerlizzi says he has been intrigued by the idea of viewing Earth as a giant living organism. "George Carlin used to do this funny bit about how humans are always scared about the end of the world," he recalls. "'The planet is fine, and it's not going anywhere, we are! The planet will shake us off like a case of bad fleas!' he'd joke. I started to think what the Earth would look like after humans disappeared. I wanted to imagine an optimistic version of dystopia, where we have the rebirth and genesis and the seeding of a planet."

DiTerlizzi says an artistic source of inspiration for Orbona was Rudolph Zallinger's famous mural at the Yale University's Peabody Museum of Natural History titled *The Age of Reptiles*, which depicts a range of dinosaurs moving about in a prehistoric landscape. "I had a poster of that painting in my bedroom when I was a kid," he says. "I loved these ancient, strange plants which are completely alien to us today. The world that Eva discovers above her sanctuary has similar, but intelligent, plants. I sent John Lasseter, Andy Harkness, and Bobs Gannaway a folder of images, and they mined it for inspiration for this world."

Harkness says he and his team wanted the world of Orbona to stand out as a huge contrast to the Sanctuary, which Eva 9 leaves after the first episode. "We leave the light, lime-green color of MUTHR and her world behind," he says. "She wakes up and knows that something weird is going on. That's what we call the Jurassic Park shot, because that's when Eva sees the world of Orbana for the first time. The whole set was built in VR, and we can see the world through Eva's eyes as we introduce all kinds of creatures that are now roaming this new, repopulated Earth."

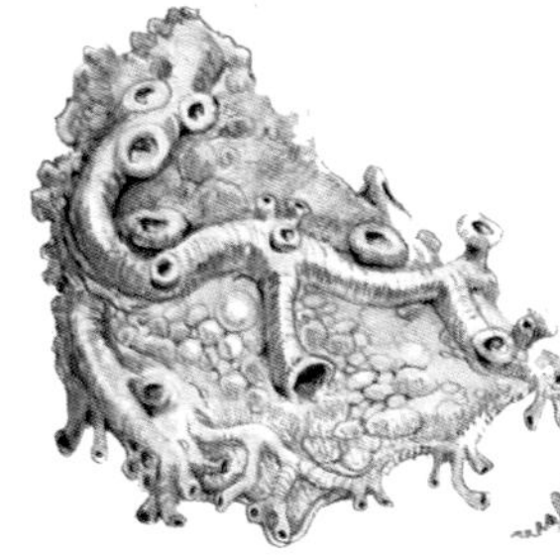

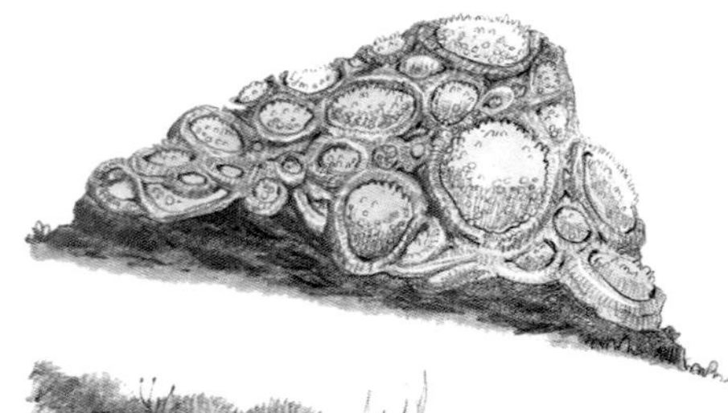

THIS SPREAD
Plants by
Nicolas Weis

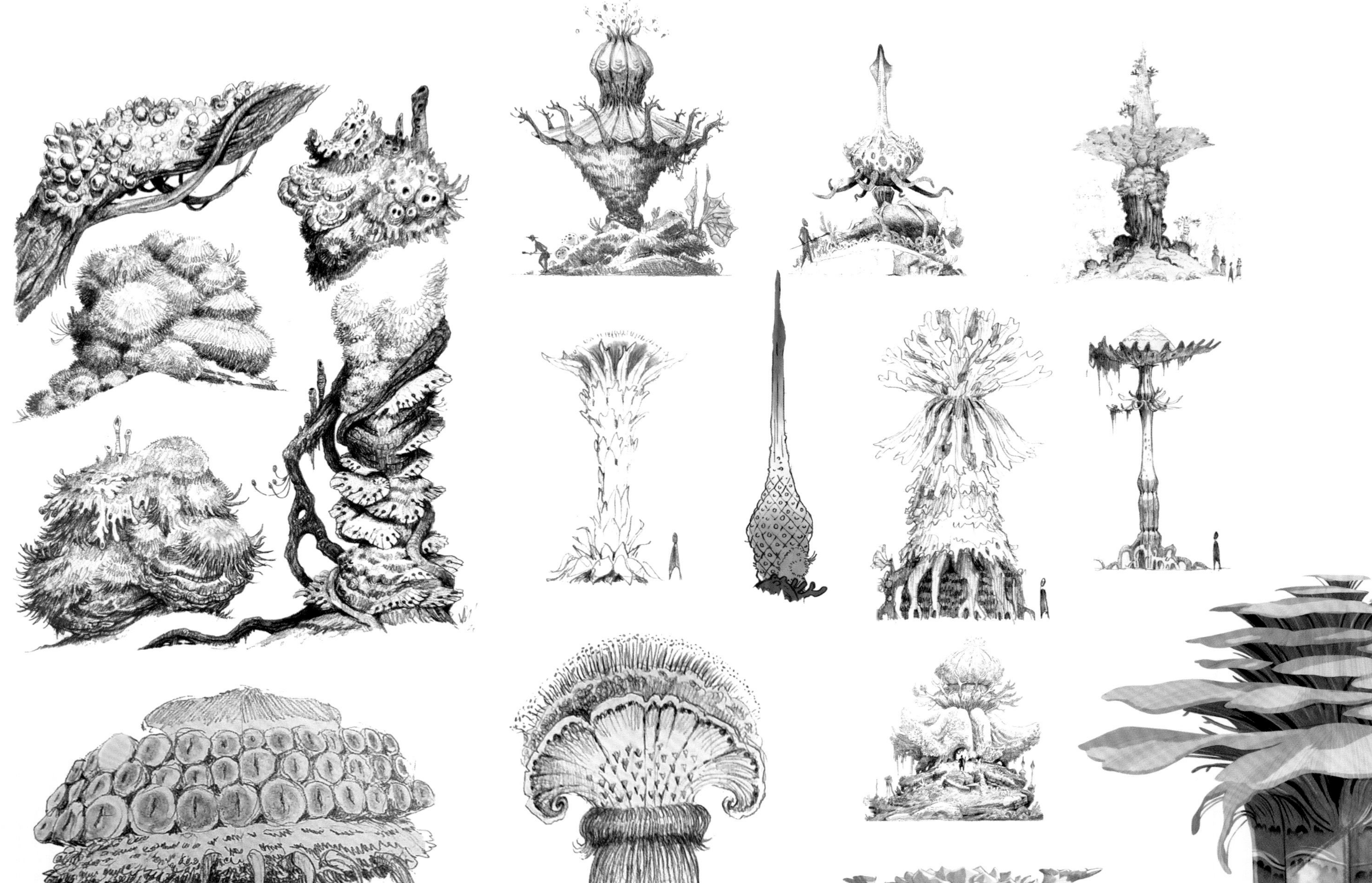

ABOVE & BELOW
Sepia plants by Nicolas Weis

FAR LEFT
Hippoplant by JJ Song

LEFT
Plants in color by JJ Song

BELOW
Artwork by Simon Baek

RIGHT
Final render

CREATURE

AIR WHALES

THE MAJESTIC FLYING WHALES OF ORBONA provide some of the most breath-taking images throughout the show. They are described as large flying organisms that travel in pods buoyed by air-sacs above their heads. Mostly gentle and harmless by nature, they play an important role in the grand confrontation between the two factions in the show's finale.

LEFT
Baby air whale sketch by Saira Vargas

BELOW
Paint artwork by Christine Kim

THIS SPREAD
Artwork by
JJ Song

CREATURE

SANDSNIPERS

RIGHT
Adult sandsniper artwork by JJ Song

BELOW
Baby sandsniper design by Ang Chen and artwork by JJ Song

THESE NATIVE CRUSTACEAN CREATURES ARE natives of Orbona. Eva 9 comes across these giant creatures several times throughout the three seasons of *WondLa*. They live in burrows under the surface and are prone to ambush their prey when they suddenly emerge. They communicate with a series of clicks and chirps with the other members of their clan. Because of her special abilities, Eva 9 can communicate with them and ask for their help. They can take on creatures that are much larger than them (Besteel, for example) because they hunt in packs.

Gannaway has a great story about how the sandsnipers found their way into the world of the book and the series. "I remember I was in Florida on vacation, and my family and I stopped by a souvenir shop that has a giant 30-foot-tall lobster sculpture in front of it," he recalls. I sent it to Tony DiTerlizzi and said, "Look what I found," and he told me that giant lobster was the inspiration for the sandsnipers in his books! That goes back to the great design philosophy of tethering things to truth so that there's a sense of reality to them. Of course, this is not a prescriptive notion, because there are many ways that animation can be done, but I subscribe to the idea that if the audience feels that something is real, they'll stop looking at it, and they'll start feeling it. I think the brain starts to connect with the image when there is some element of familiarity. The audience will sniff out something that's fake whether it's the textures that don't look right or if the characters don't carry the right weight. So, that's why it was important to get things to carry elements of truth so there's no wall between your audience and the characters."

CREATURE

TURNFINS

THIS PAGE
Sketches by Saira Vargas

THIS PAGE
Color artwork by Maliheh Rahrovan

LOCATION

LACUS

OPPOSITE PAGE
Artwork by Dominique Louis

BELOW
Artwork by Andy Harkness and Kalina Murat

LACUS IS A CHARMING FISHING VILLAGE LOCATED on the coast of Lake Concors. Its residents are mostly Halcyonus, who are close relatives of Caeruleans. In the first season of the show, Eva 9, MUTHR and Rovender spend the night at the Haveport family's hut before they begin their trek to Solas.

"Everything in Lacus is based on fishing motifs," says John Lasseter. "There is always a logic behind the design. We wanted each place to be different so that the audience feels like they are taken to worlds they have never seen before. We did a lot of research on the history of alien characters on film and TV, including *Star Trek* and *Star Wars*, but we wanted to carve our own way, and it all started with Tony's drawings."

Lasseter says he wanted the audience to fall in love with the natural beauty of Lacus. "The goal is to make them want to book a week's vacation to this world even though it's not a real place," he adds. "Tony bases his designs on things that fascinate him and those awe-inspiring alien trees are all inspired by things that he has come across. Andy Harkness and his team then evolved the book's illustration for the series. I recall when my wife first saw the show, she absolutely fell in love with the locations and said she wished she could visit Lacus."

DiTerlizzi says one of his main initial sources of inspiration for Lacus when he came upon an unusual natural phenomenon during one of his daily walks in Florida. "There's a very small insect called the gall wasp which lays its eggs inside a twig or some fruit," he says. "But the wasp also injects a chemical inside the host plant which causes it to grow extra tissue around the eggs. The plant mutates around the tree galls, and the little wasps live off those growths until it pupates and digs its way out. So, those weird natural growths were what I used as inspiration for the beautiful city of Lacus!"

Harkness says Lacus was the absolute craziest and most fun set he had ever designed in his career (and he has worked on movies such as *Moana*,

Zootopia, and *Vivo*, and won an Emmy for his work on the Disney special, *Prep & Landing*) "I probably spent six to eight hours a day in VR for about four months straight," he says. "Lacus was a set, within a set, within a set! I was so grateful John Lasseter bought into this idea of designing the world using VR. I think I went a little crazy! I started to believe Lacus was a real place!"

Harkness explains that the plants of this location are based on a real tree species called a hornbeam and the aloe vera plant. "We gave [Lacus' trees] these giant asparagus-like stems that shoot up," he says. "The living trees are the basis of the architecture of this world, and the canopy forms the city of Lacus. Everything's alive, and nothing is killed and cut off. The houses are made of some type of mushroom—not like a house in the Smurf village, but a lot cooler. They empty them out and carve out the center, and the roots of the tree become part of the organic architecture of the homes. The center of Lacus is a freshwater pond that is the home of the fish. The marketplace surrounds this pond. When you walk through town and around the pond, you'll pass a bar and Caruncle's shop. I have spent so much time there that I feel like this town is my hometown now!"

THIS SPREAD
Concept art

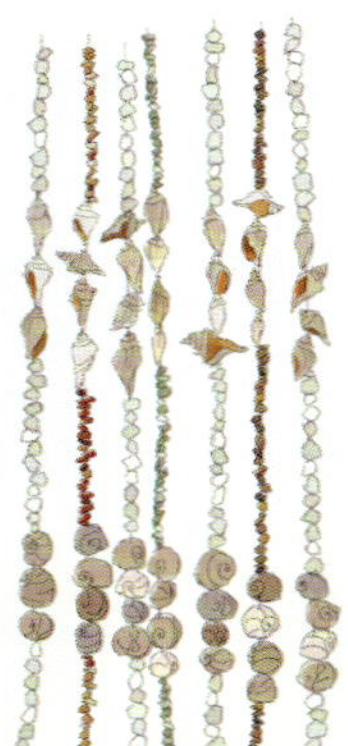

LEFT
Chimes by Julie Chon

RIGHT & BELOW
Paint artwork and renders by Andy Harkness and JJ Song

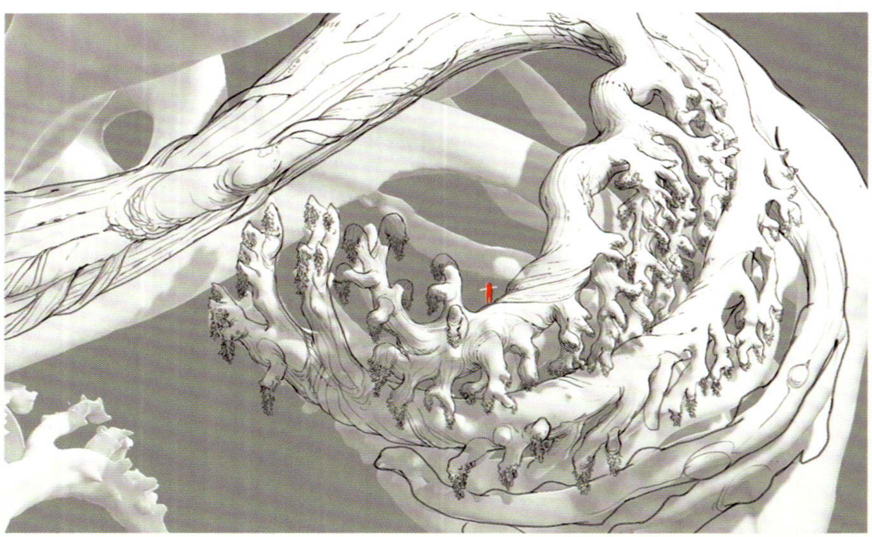

ABOVE
Signs by Kalina Murat

ABOVE
Signs by Craig Foster

RIGHT
Paint artwork of shop by Andy Harkness

BELOW
Shells by Christine Kim

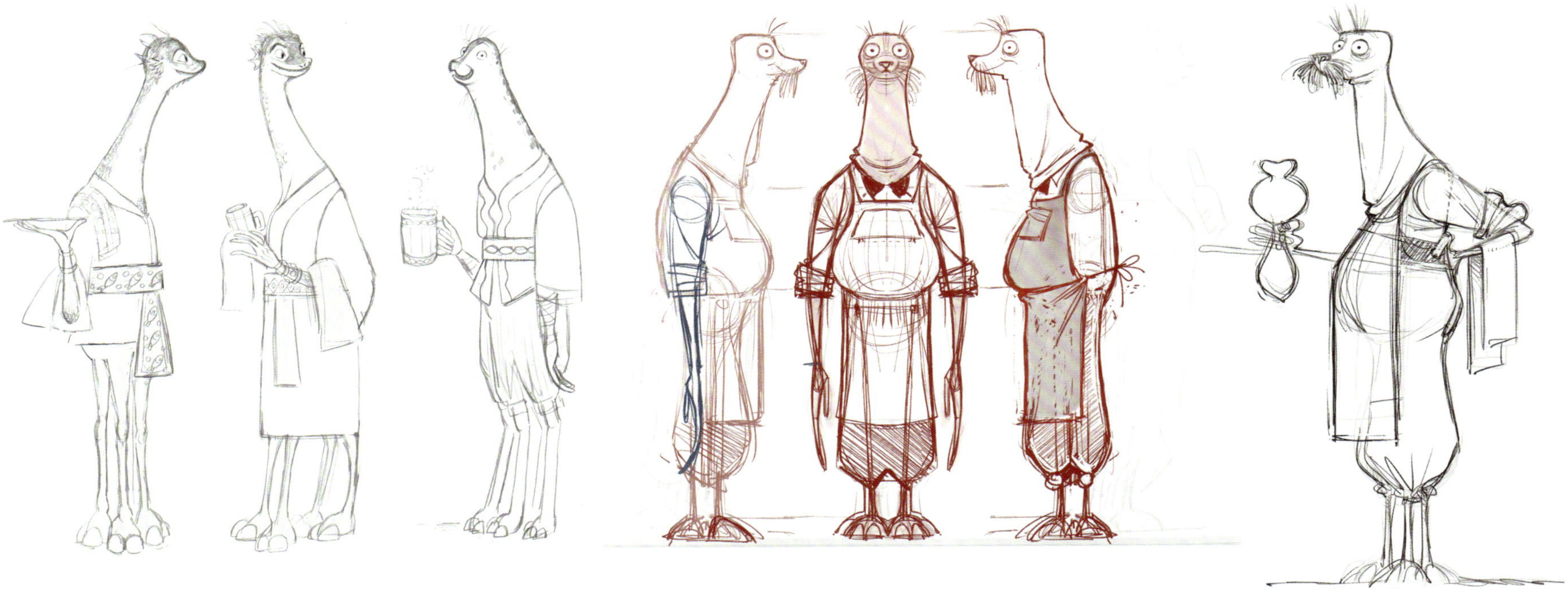

TEXTILE PATTERNS

TOP
Mirthian sketches by Yaou Chen

BOTTOM
Mirthian costume by Neysa Bove

FAR LEFT
Cups by Christine Kim

BELOW
Bar design by Andy Harkness and paint artwork by Simon Baek

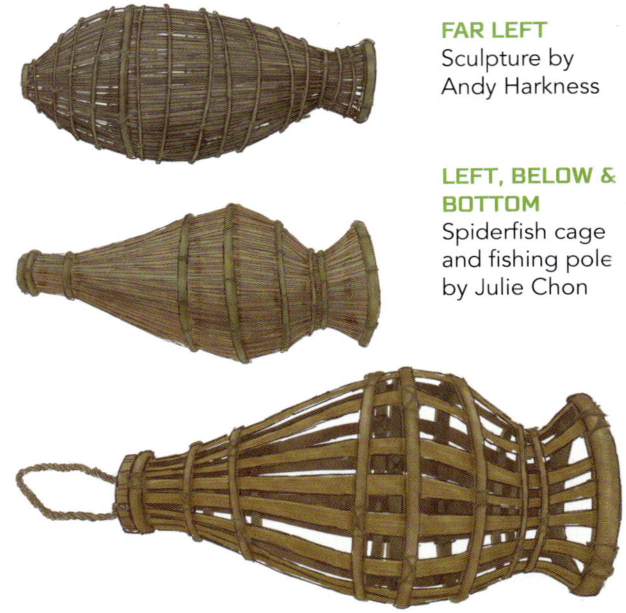

FAR LEFT
Sculpture by Andy Harkness

LEFT, BELOW & BOTTOM
Spiderfish cage and fishing pole by Julie Chon

LEFT
Spiderfish racecourse artwork by Andy Harkness

BOTTOM
Amber design by Simon Baek

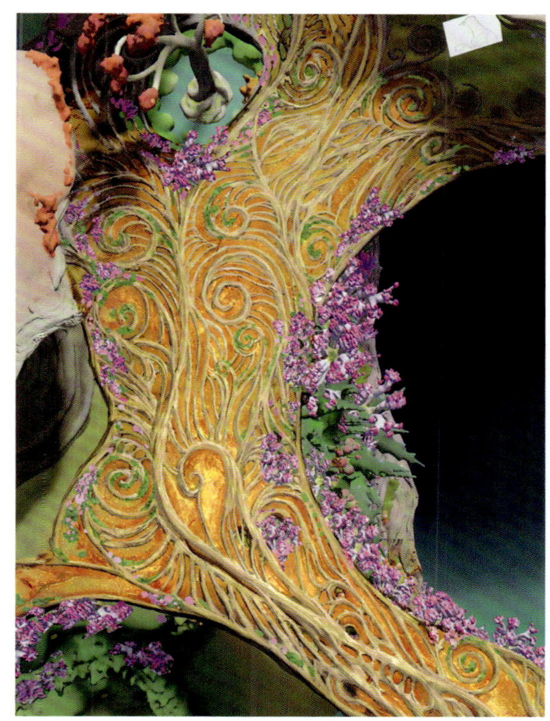

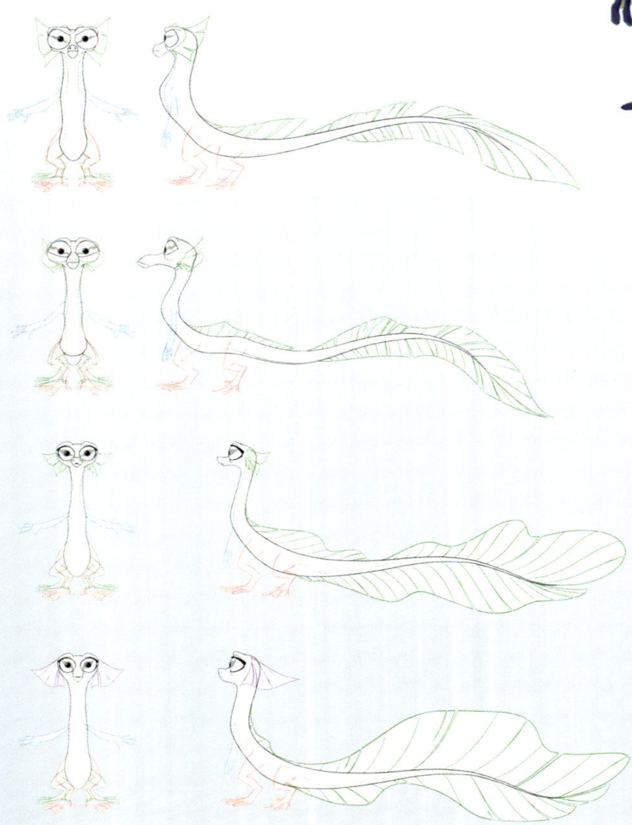

LEFT
Sketch by Saira Vargas

BELOW LEFT
Variants by Chris Ables

BELOW
Paint artwork by Maliheh Rahrovan

RIGHT
Sketch by Saira Vargas

CREATURE

SPIDERFISH

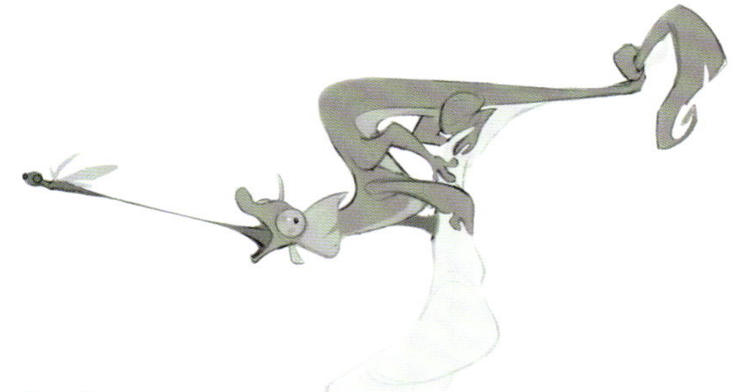

WITH A LONG, LEAN BODY SIMILAR TO A BASILISK lizard, a tadpole-like tail, and pufferfish ears, the colorful spiderfish is one of Lacus' most exotic and important creatures. The annual spiderfish race plays a major part in the first season's third episode in which Eva 9 wins 300 "shellacks" by betting on Crusty, an unlikely winner in the race.

As artist and designer Maliheh Rahrovan explains, "Working on the spiderfish characters was such a fun assignment. Like all the other characters and locations of *WondLa*, we spent a lot of time looking at real-world references and images from frogs, fish, and lizards in water. I was very happy to find some video footage of a type of lizard that runs on water. At the studio, we constantly try to iterate and build upon the previous designs. It's all about improving what we did before and coming up with the best version of an idea or a design."

ABOVE
Sketch by Saira Vargas

LEFT
Paint artwork by Maliheh Rahrovan

BELOW
Early sketches by Maliheh Rahrovan

CHARACTER

CARUNCLE

OPPOSITE PAGE
Artwork by Chris Ables

RIGHT
Paint artwork by JJ Song

BELOW
Artwork by Chris Ables

EVA 9 AND ROVENDER MEET CARUNCLE, a fast-talking and crafty alien trader and salvager in the first season. Voiced by Pixar veteran actor John Ratzenberger, the Lacus resident has a big head, heavy body, and skinny legs and arms like a mini T-Rex. He is fond of playing an old barrel grinder and sells long-gone human artifacts, furniture, and knick-knacks (including salt and pepper shakers, stop signs, antique furniture, filing cabinets, even a 1950s-era jukebox) in his shop. Rovender calls it "his palace of junk," but Caruncle refers to them as exotic curiosities collected from all over Orbona. If you look closely, you can even find Leonardo da Vinci's *Mona Lisa* (it could be the real thing or a knock-off—who knows) right next to a velvet painting of dogs playing poker in the background!

"Caruncle is a great source of comic relief," says Senoo. "He will be very charming and ask you to show you everything he has to offer if he thinks you are going to spend some money. However, if he finds out you don't have money, he will kick you out of his shop immediately!"

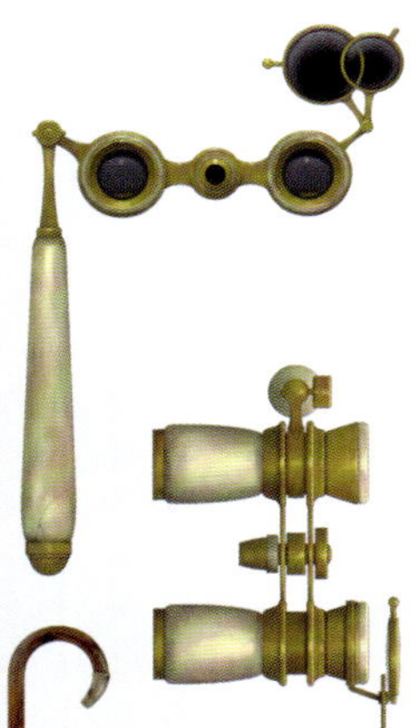

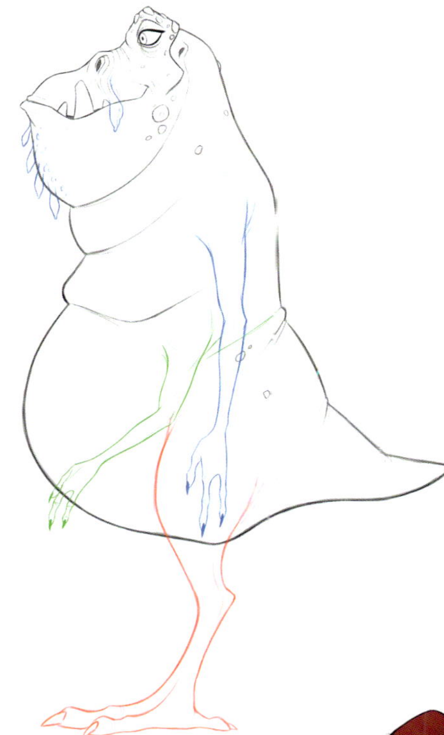

OPPOSITE PAGE
Artwork by Andy Harkness and paint by Simon Baek

THIS PAGE
Sketches by Paul Westacott

BELOW
Signs by Andrew Taylor

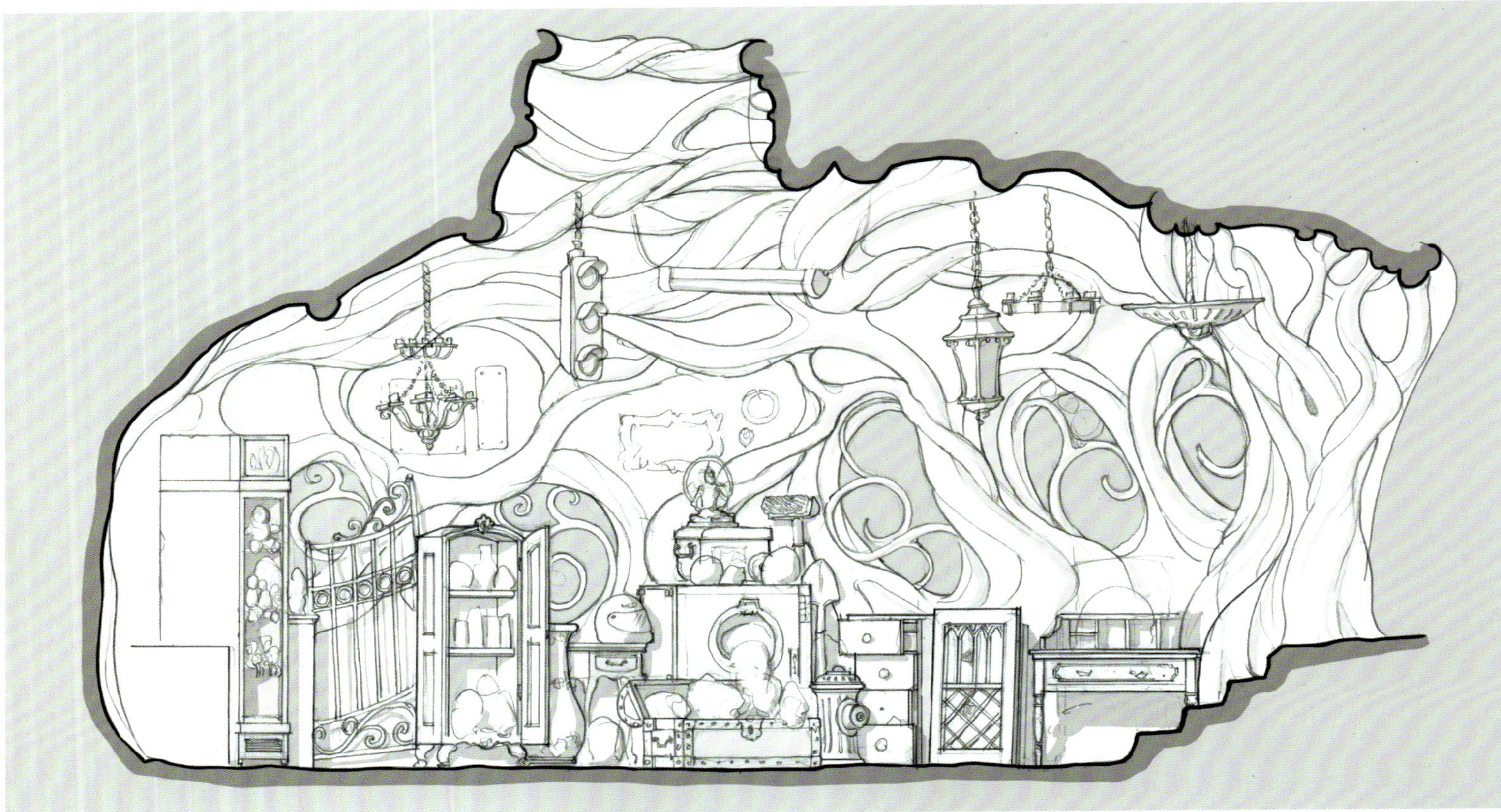

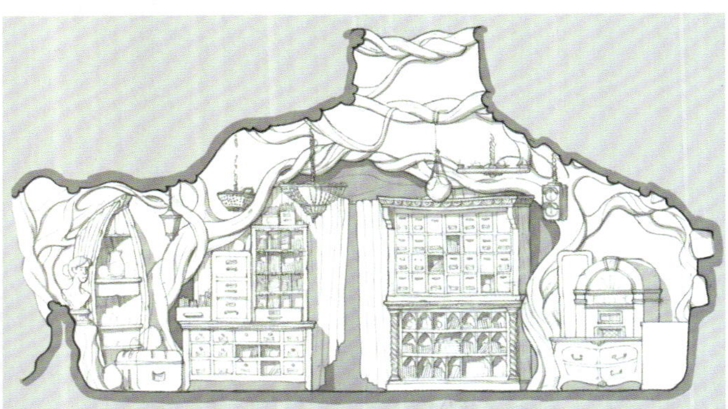

Do not hold doors
Do not lean on door

RIGHT
Costume artwork by Neysa Bove

BELOW
Artwork by Saira Vargas

CHARACTER

HAVEPORT FAMILY

THE HAVEPORT FAMILY FIRST APPEAR WHEN Eva 9, Rovender, and MUTHR seek refuge in their warm and welcoming home in Lacus. Hostia and her husband Fiscian are old friends of Rovender's and they help them as they are trying to escape Besteel. Kind Halcyonus aliens, they are in sharp contrast with the some of the more hostile aliens and the cold, orderly world of Cadmus and the Sanctuaries. Their house is the perfect example of the typical homes of Lacus, completely organic and made in the hollow areas of the region's giant trees. Their loose-fitting brown robes and outfits are also inspired by indigenous American cultures, with some designs resembling shellfish or some spiderfish patterns sprinkled as subtle reminders of their background.

"I remember reading the book and getting such a great visual for the Haveports' home," says Harkness. "There's a little room before the main room where they take the shoes off and they wash their feet out of respect before they enter the main area of the house. The color palette is warm and because it feels like a new home for Eva, everything is in shades of oranges and yellows. The upper bedroom is where the kids' bedroom is. If you look out of the window, you can see Darius's house."

THIS PAGE
Artwork by Saira Vargas and Neysa Bove

LOCATION

HALLYONUS HOUSE

LEFT
Front door by Michele Graybeal

BELOW LEFT
Lounge by Armand Serrano and JJ Song

BELOW
Wall artwork by Michele Graybeal

THIS PAGE
Artwork by Andy Harkness and Dominique Louis

THIS PAGE
Sketches by Yaou Chen

CHARACTER

DARIUS

EVA 9 MEETS DARIUS (VOICED BY THE ENIGMATIC Shohreh Aghdashloo), an ancient Arsian alien who has the power to see the future, in the fourth episode of the first season. Darius travelled to Orbona during the Great Migration. The oracle's visions are less of a certainty, and more of a "probable" future. Darius is Arius's sister, who is known for making textiles that reveal knowledge of the future, but she requires payment of a dream first. They are both reclusive and cryptic. They have the power to experience the past of the planet, and so they feel all the pain, trauma, and the eventual destruction of Earth, which makes them afraid and distrusting of all humans. In the book, Darius and Arius are Zin and Loroc's sisters.

LEFT
Artwork by Neysa Bove

BELOW LEFT
Headpieces by Yaou Chen

BELOW
Sketches by Christine Kim

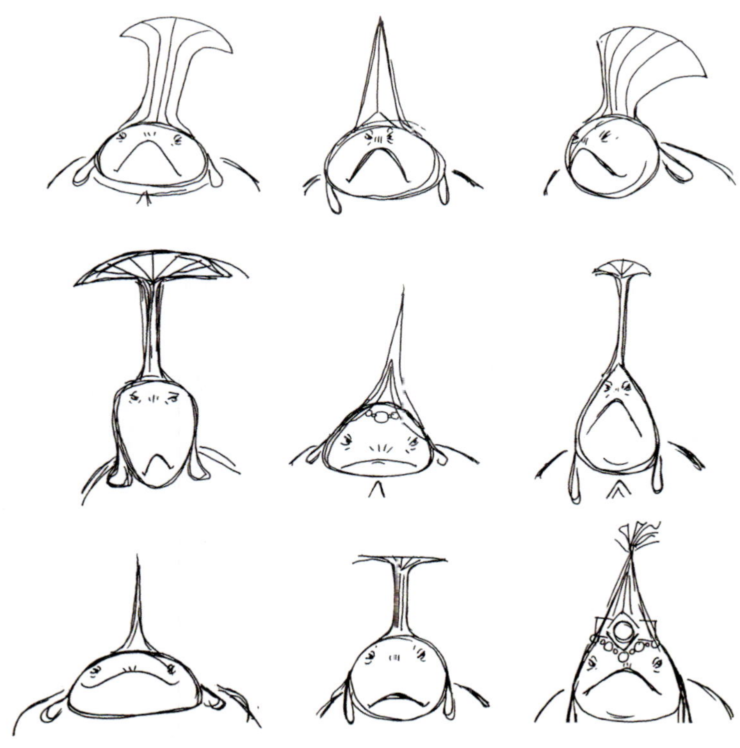

THIS PAGE
Artwork by
Simon Baek

THIS PAGE
Artwork by Andy Harkness

LOCATION

SOLAS

OPPOSITE PAGE
Artwork by Armand Serrano and Maliheh Rahrovan

BELOW
Artwork by Armand Serrano

BOTTOM RIGHT
Artwork by Armand Serrano

A GLISTENING GREEN CITY LOCATED ON THE coast of Lake Concors, Solas is home to Queen Ojo's palace, the Royal Menagerie and the Royal Museum. You can reach the city via ferry from Lacus.

"I was definitely inspired by The Emerald City in *The Wizard of Oz* when I wrote about Solas," recalls DiTerlizzi. "I was also looking at a lot of Ernst Haeckel, a turn-of-the-century German artist and naturalist who is famous for his detailed drawings of plankton and other similar organisms. I bought a couple of his books and there was a section in one of his books that had a chandelier which looked like a jellyfish. I thought this kind of design of 'alien nouveau art' would be perfect for Solas. I put a big folder of his art together and sent it to the design team; they went nuts and went off and created the world of Queen Ojo and her castle."

Andy Harkness explains that the castle is seen as the peak of alien technology. "We were hugely inspired by art deco and the architectural masterpieces of Antonio Gaudí," he points out. "If you look at their take on art deco, there's a symmetry to things, but it's also very organic and has close ties to nature. All their buildings are inspired by Orbona's flora and fauna. We won't really see gold colors again except for the car they take from Solas to the Grasslands. My good friend Armand Serrano designed this whole set beautifully in VR, and I did the color for it."

BELOW
Artwork by
Simon Baek

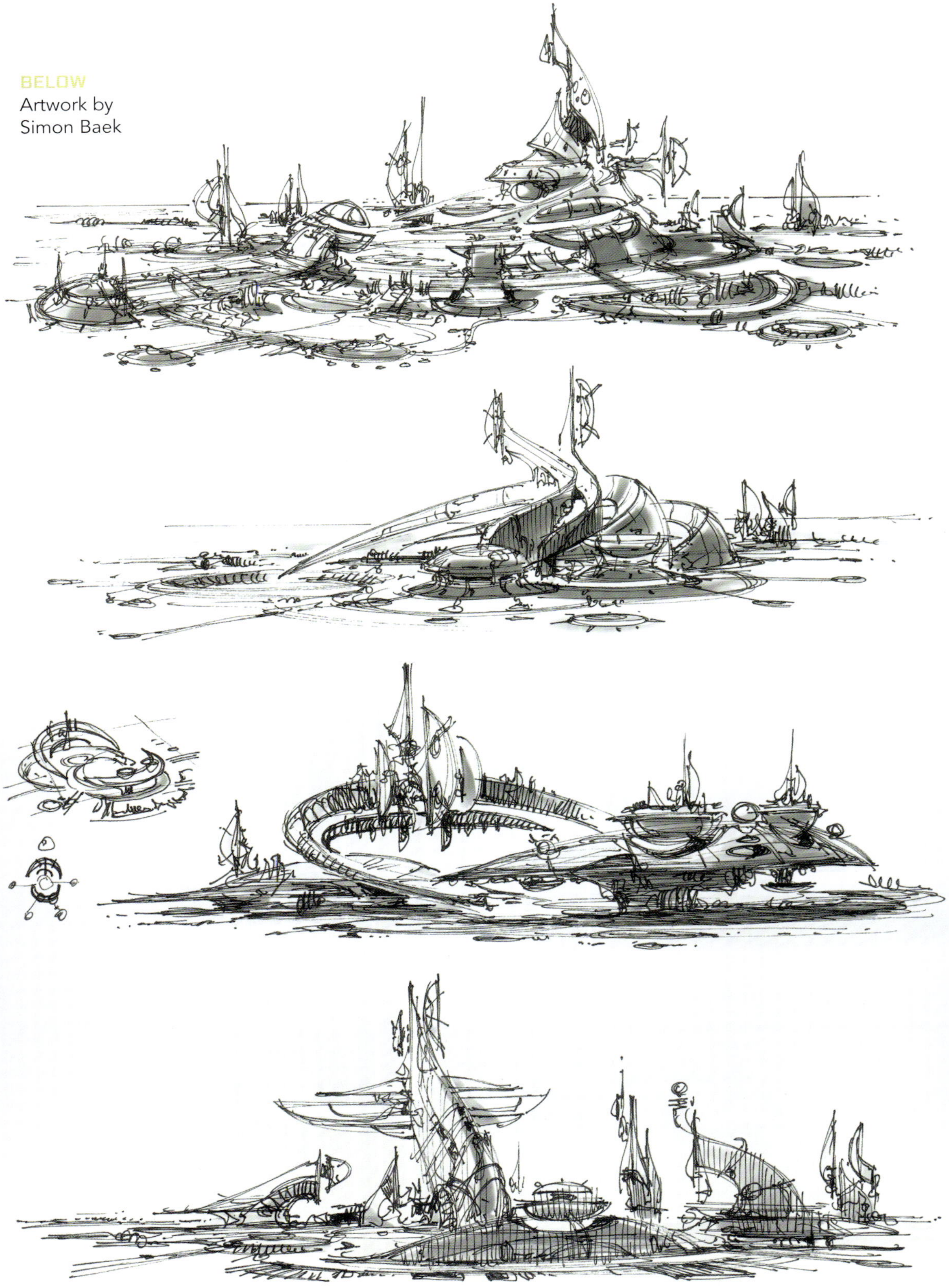

RIGHT
Artwork by
Simon Baek

ABOVE
Dome and garden by Armand Serrano and Nobuteru Sasagawa, ceiling design by Simon Baek

RIGHT
Entrance by Marc Gabbana

OPPOSITE PAGE
Artwork by Armand Serrano

OPPOSITE PAGE
Paint artwork by
Michele Graybeal

RIGHT & BELOW
Door by
Kalina Murat

FAR RIGHT
Columns by
Marc Gabbana

BOTTOM
Artwork by
Jeff Wagner

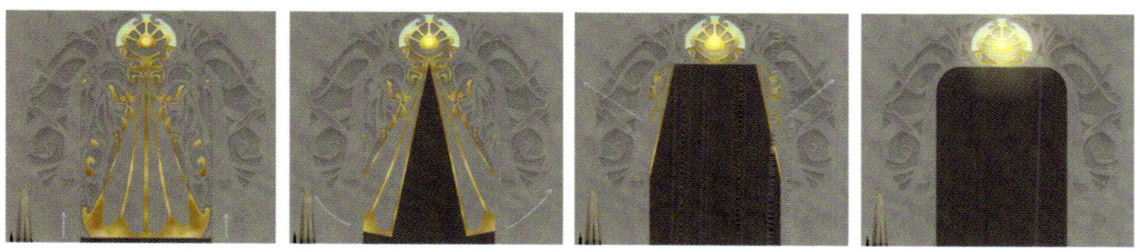

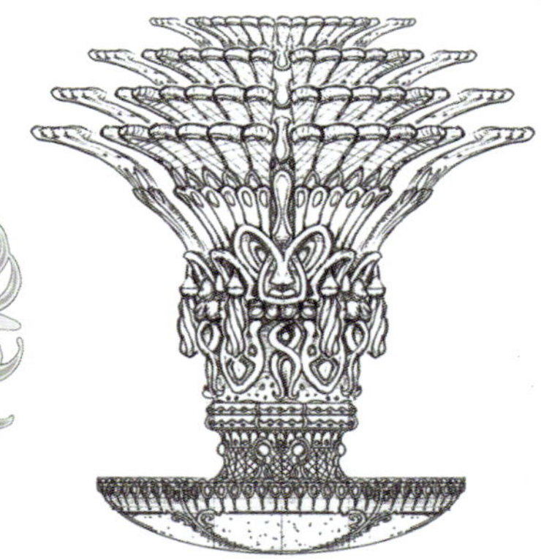

RIGHT
Throne by Marc
Gabbana and
Armand Serrano

BELOW
Artwork by Jeff Wagner and Simon Baek

RIGHT
Guards by Michele Graybeal

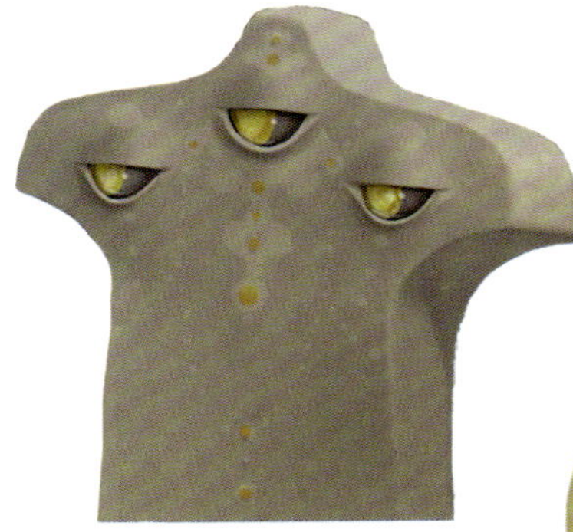

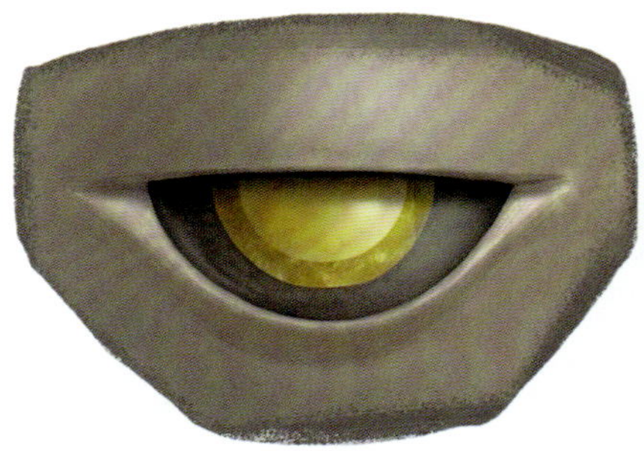

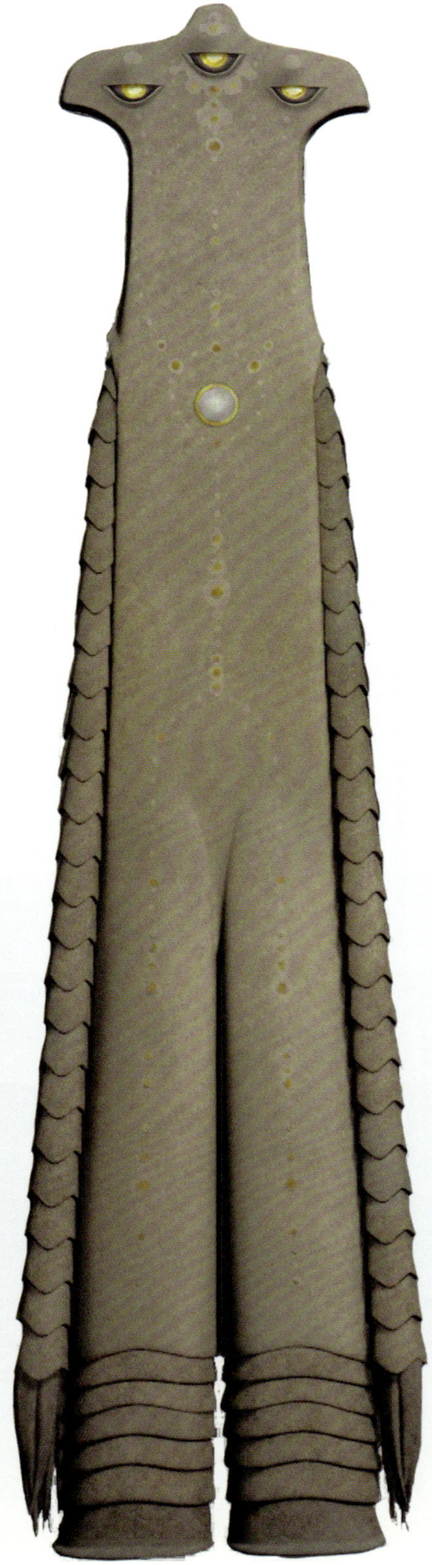

RIGHT
Robot, pinball machines, and toy dispenser by Julie Chon

BELOW
Goldfish artwork by Richard Lee

BOTTOM RIGHT
Lamp by Nicolas Weis and container by Kalina Murat

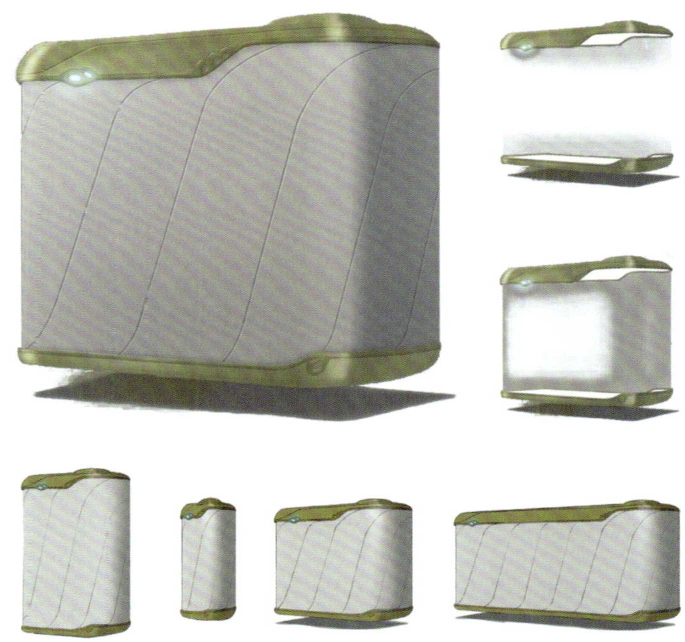

RIGHT
Artwork by
Chris Ables

BELOW
Artwork
by Sylvain
Deboissey

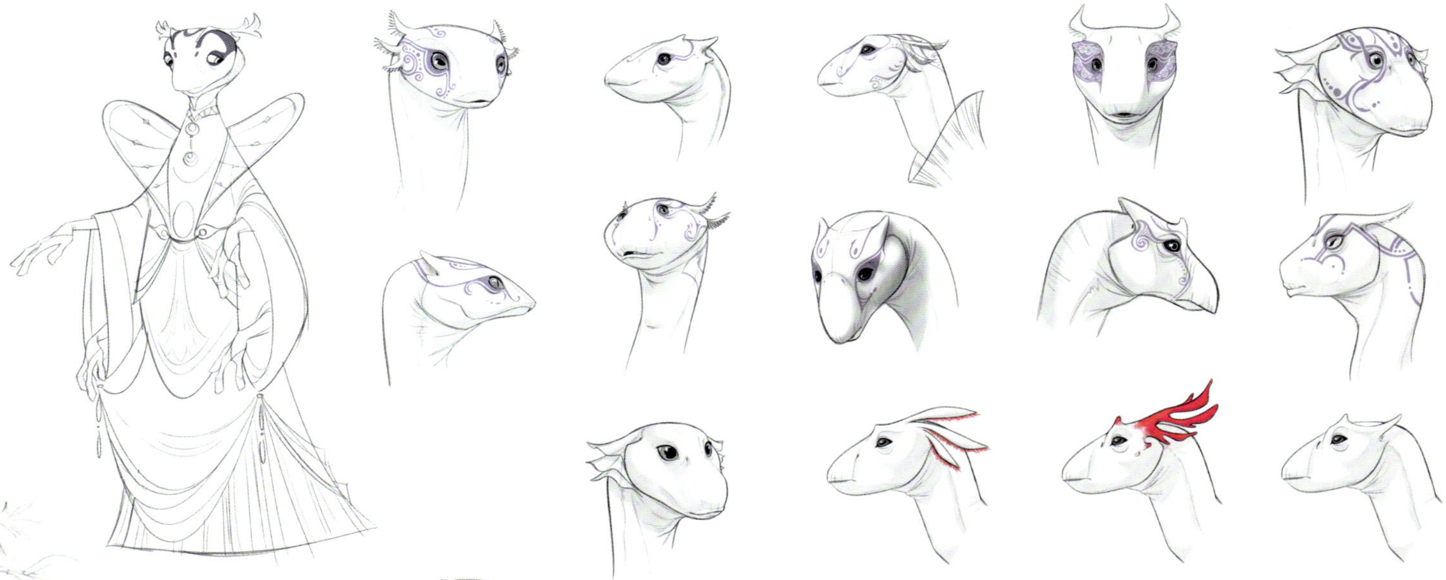

CHARACTER

QUEEN OJO

THE ALABASTER-SKINNED YOUNG QUEEN OJO (voiced by Sarah Hollis) is the leader of the immigrant alien race who were forced to abandon their own planet and land on a ravaged Earth in their giant ark. She is graceful and majestic, and her face and droopy ears wouldn't look out of place on an animated goat or a lamb. She lives in a cavernous castle in Solas.

"The young Queen's design is truly beautiful, and her voice is also perfect," says Lasseter. "She and Eva 9 immediately emotionally connect in one single episode because they are around the same age, and you can see how they bond for life."

Neysa Bove says she was hugely influenced by what women wore during the Art Nouveau period (approximately 1890-1910) when she began to think about Queen Ojo's long, flowing and delicately embroidered gowns. "Women of that era were tired of wearing restrictive bustles and corsets that created this hourglass figure," she explains. "They started wearing these tea dresses, which are very loose on top. I drew her with something similar, but with a bit of a tighter skirt in the bottom, which was borrowing a bit from the 1920s and was ahead of its time. I also added new pieces on like the shoulder cage and the tiara. That's the beauty of creating a culture that doesn't exist: you can bring in other elements and flourishes to add your own special twist. The cage that she wears is made of gold, inset with opals. I thought those gems looked magical and iridescent, and perfectly regal for a queen. She was one of my favorite characters to costume."

LEFT
Artwork by Neysa Bove

BELOW
Artwork by Sylvain Deboissey

BOTTOM
Final stills

ABOVE
Artwork by Michele Graybeal

Yuriko Senoo also brings up Ojo as one of her favorites. "She has these long eyelashes and graceful moments as she moves around in her flowing drapery," Senoo says. "We had to do a lot of tests to figure out whether we should overlap her long eyelashes or whether it would be too distracting. In the end we just kept them stiff so that we could really focus on her facial expressions instead of her lashes. I know the character effects department also had to work very hard on the flowing drapery to bring the designs to animated life, but the results of everyone's hard work paid off because she's absolutely gorgeous."

Josh Herrig agrees. "We had to put both Tony DiTerlizzi's original book designs and the series' designers work through rigorous animation, rigging, and shading considerations to find what sorts of assets would fit the pace we needed to animate at. Long flowing dresses or long hair or complicated rigging and character effects were always a consideration during production. We had to determine if they were totally essential to the storytelling. In some cases, they were more than essential so we would collaborate on a plan and decide exactly where we would focus that energy. Queen Ojo was a great example where we felt it was essential to embrace her regal nature and ensure she had a flowing gold gown, very long eye lashes with pearls in them, and fur and feathers."

BELOW
Final still

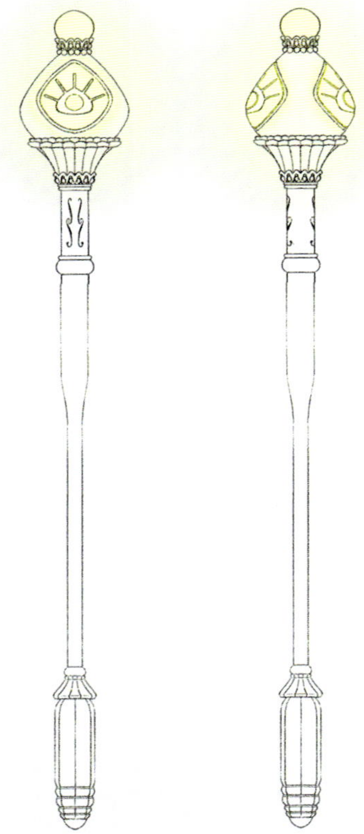

LEFT & BELOW
Sceptre by Kalina Murat

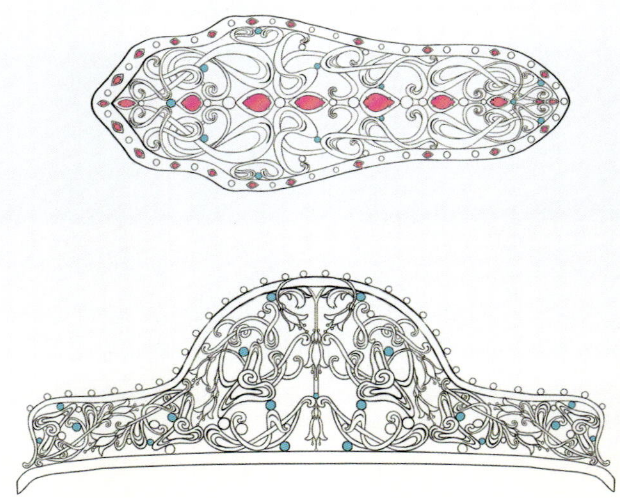

BOTTOM
Crown and shoulder piece by Neysa Bove

ZIN

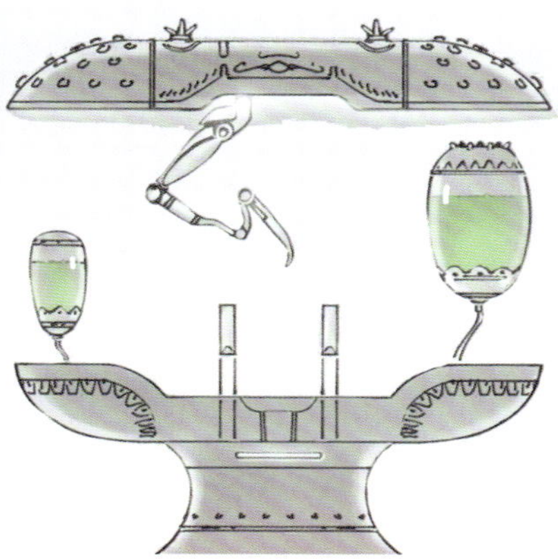

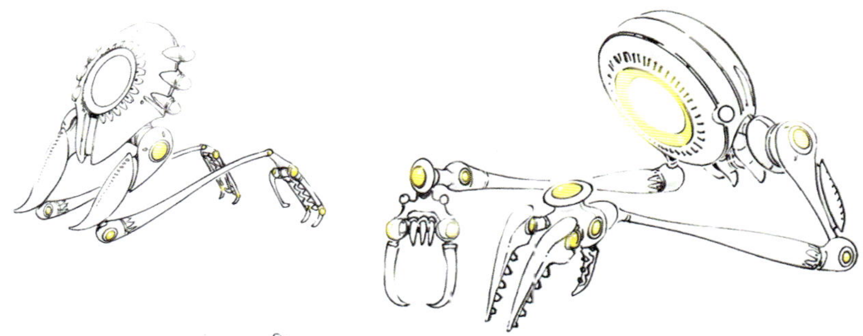

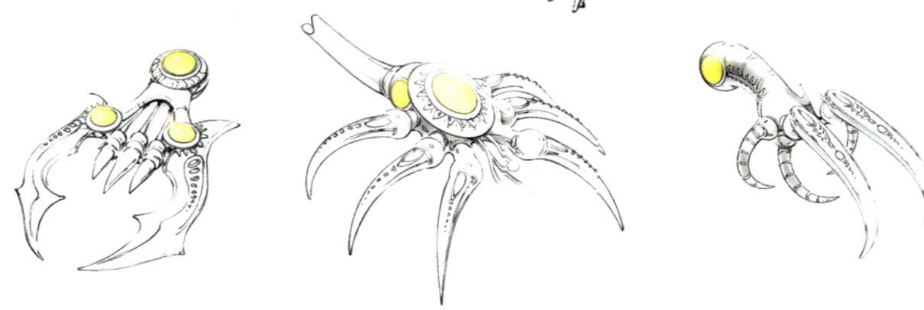

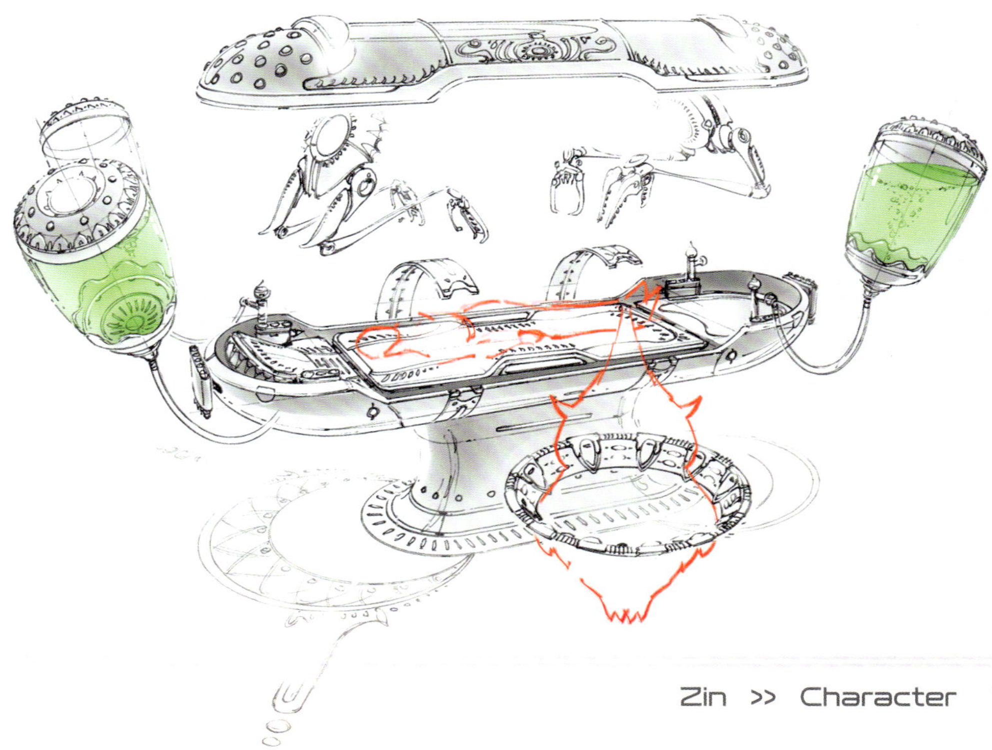

FAR LEFT
Zin artwork by Kalina Murat and Michele Graybeal

LEFT & BELOW
Torture device by Marc Gabbana

LOCATION

GRASSLAND

OPPOSITE PAGE
Artwork by
Michele Graybeal

BELOW CENTER
Lichen detail by
JJ Song

BELOW
Artwork by
Andy Harkness

AFTER VISITING THE LUSH AND VERDANT WORLDS of Lacus and Solas, Eva 9 and MUTHR ride the Goldfish car to the drier regions of Orbana on their way to New York City. According to production designer Andy Harkness, the grasslands all look like those in Nebraska. "There's nothing really dead in Orbana, but this area is imagined as Nebraska or one of the Great Lakes in the US. They cross the grassland in the sixth episode of the first season, and there is nothing too unusual here. If you are eating sushi, you will need some ginger to cleanse your palette. Visually, that's what we get here. We do a reset before they head over to New York. It's beautiful and sunny here, but they'll be getting dark clouds once they get closer to the city."

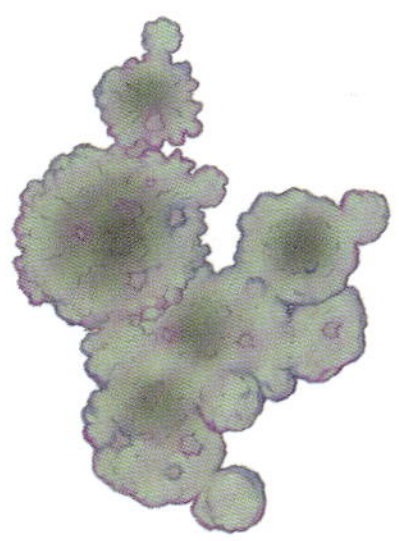

LOCATION

GW BRIDGE

THE EDGE-OF-YOUR-SEAT CROSSING OF THE ravaged George Washington Bridge in the sixth episode of the first season allows Eva 9 to truly learn the value of MUTHR, Rovender, and Otto. She is hopeful to find other humans at this point, and New York City holds a lot of promise as she and her friends look at it in the distance from the bridge.

"There are clouds coming in, and we were referencing San Francisco and the Golden Gate Bridge," says Harkness. "Initially, the colors are bright, and we didn't want to suddenly shift the colors, but gradually we see that everything's falling apart. There's all the dust on the ground from the fragments of the moon that have hit the Earth's surface."

The design team did a lot of research to get all the details of the famous New York Library down. That's when Eva 9 discovers the true meaning of *WondLa* and realizes that the paper she thinks is a clue to the location of other humans is only the torn title page of *The Wonderful Wizard of Oz*. "She hits rock bottom, and we have another visual color switch as the battle takes place between MUTHR and Besteel, everything turns orange. The sun is lower now, and burning through the dust, and we have this orange glow cast on everything, intensifying the colors and complementing the story as it reaches one of its emotional peaks."

OPPOSITE PAGE
Artwork by Armand Serrano and Paul Westacott

LEFT
Artwork by Armand Serrano

BELOW
Artwork by Roy Santua, Armand Serrano, and Paul Westacott

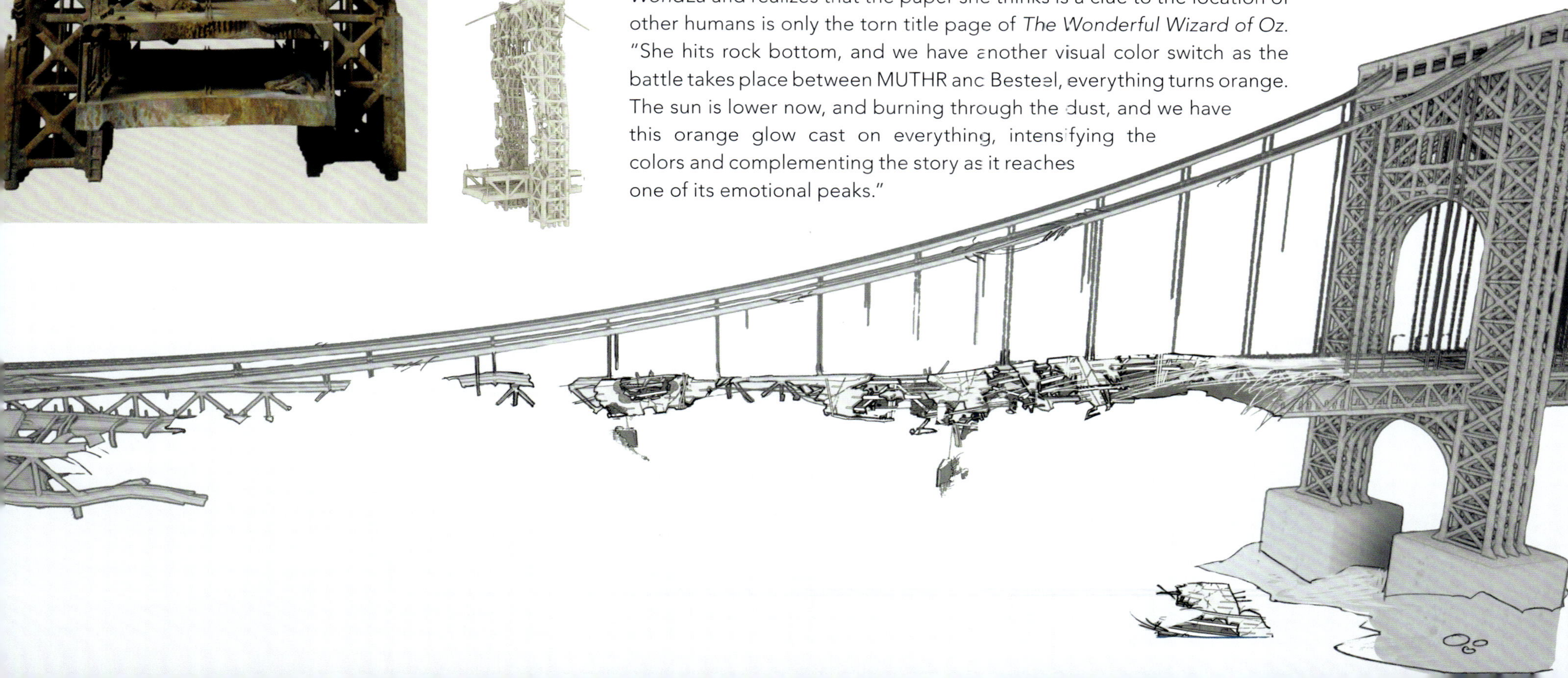

THIS SPREAD
Artwork by
Michele Graybeal

LOCATION

NEW YORK

FAR LEFT
Artwork by
Michele Graybeal

LEFT
Artwork by
Roy Santua

BELOW
Artwork by
Armand Serrano

THIS PAGE
Artwork by
Armand Serrano

THIS SPREAD
Artwork by
Dominique Louis

LEFT & BELOW
Artwork by
Simon Baek

BOTTOM & RIGHT
Artwork by
Kuba Kozlowski

THIS SPREAD
Artwork by
Martin Bergquist

FAR LEFT
Artwork by Juan Pablo López

LEFT & BELOW
Face study by Chris Ables

CHARACTER

HAILEY

AFTER HER EXPERIENCES IN NEW YORK CITY, Eva 9 meets Hailey: a cautious teenage boy around her age. He mistrusts alien lifeforms, and so is surprised by Eva 9's friendship with them and her brave attitude. Along with Vanpa, they take Eva 9 to New Attica to meet with Cadmus. Hailey's father was killed during his escape from the city. Hailey has good mechanical skills and loves flying around and retrieving people with his ship, which is called the Bijou. Hailey and his grandfather, Vanpa, live on the outskirts of New Attica.

LEFT & BELOW LEFT Artwork by Chris Ables

BELOW Portrait and turnaround by Michele Graybeal

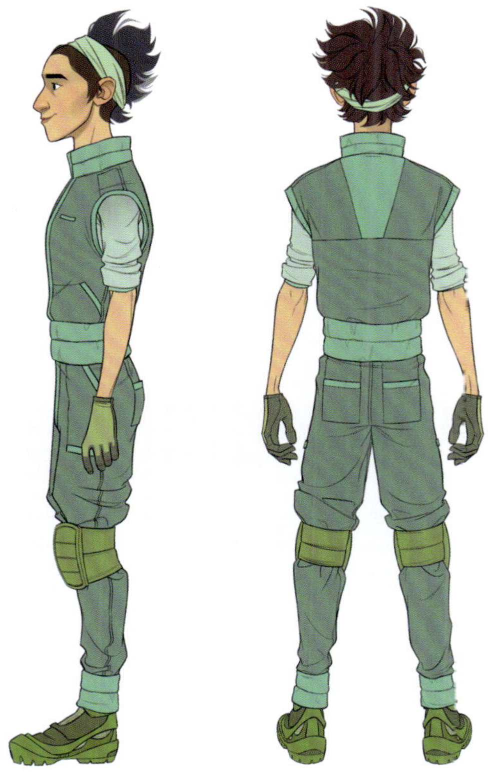

THIS SPREAD
Artwork by
Chris Ables

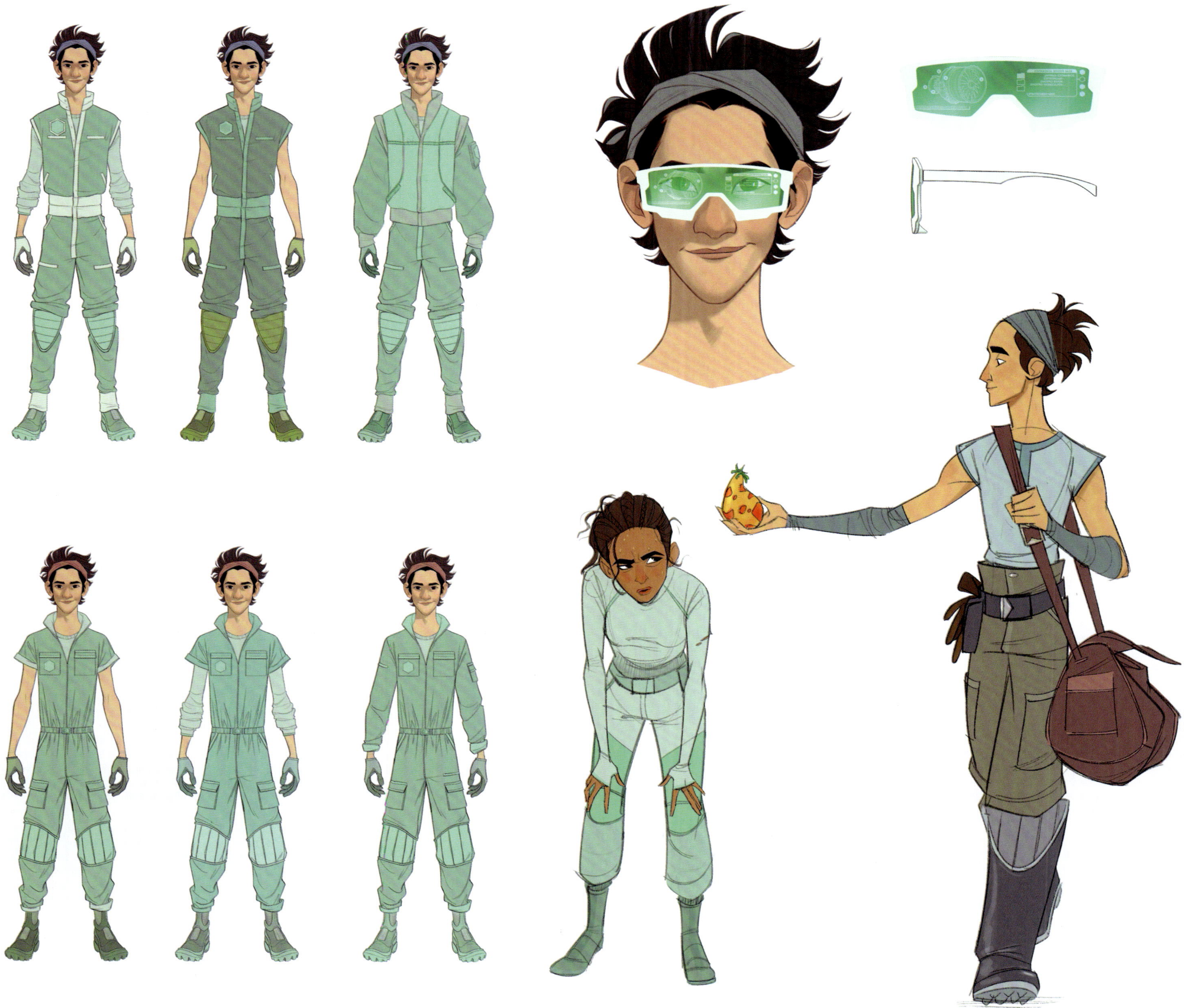

CHARACTER

VANPA

RIGHT
Artwork by Juan Pablo López

BELOW
Artwork by Chris Ables

BELOW RIGHT
Final stills

VANPA IS A CHEERFUL, SALT-OF-THE-EARTH older man who sounds like an old moonshiner from the Ozarks. He has an unwieldy grey beard, a few missing teeth, and a shiny metal prosthetic leg—which he likes to call his 'pepper grinder'. "Vanpa is a very grounded, stable character who's been around for too long," says Harkness. "He's been through it all so doesn't really take anything too seriously. He stands in stark contrast with the other people of New Attica, who all have perfect hair and clothing."

THIS PAGE
Artwork by Paul Westacott and Michele Graybeal

LOCATION

NEW ATTICA

ACCORDING TO DITERLIZZI'S BOOKS, NEW ATTICA was constructed entirely underground but was later moved into an excavated pit covered by an atmospheric membrane on which a blue sky is projected. In later years, the city was moved above ground and repopulated with human clones.

To visualize the futuristic utopia of New Attica, the production relied on the expertise of acclaimed artist, designer, and art director Marc Gabbana, whose film credits include *Star Wars: The Phantom Menace*, *Star Wars: Episode II – Attack of the Clones*, *The Matrix Reloaded*, and *War of the Worlds*. "We had a short time to build New Attica," recalls Harkness. "I've never worked on a project that we are working just ahead of and right alongside the writers. In some ways, it was really exciting. We would sit with the writers on Zoom and brainstorm this world together. There was an easy flow of information and decision-making between the writing and the visuals. After we had a pretty good rough idea of what we wanted, we went to Marc Gabbana and he designed the sets for us. He does all old-school, hardcore structural drawings. He and modeler Richard Lee worked hand in hand to build all of it to make sure it all functioned."

OPPOSITE PAGE
Artwork by Simon Baek

BELOW
Artwork by Richard Lee and Marc Gabbana

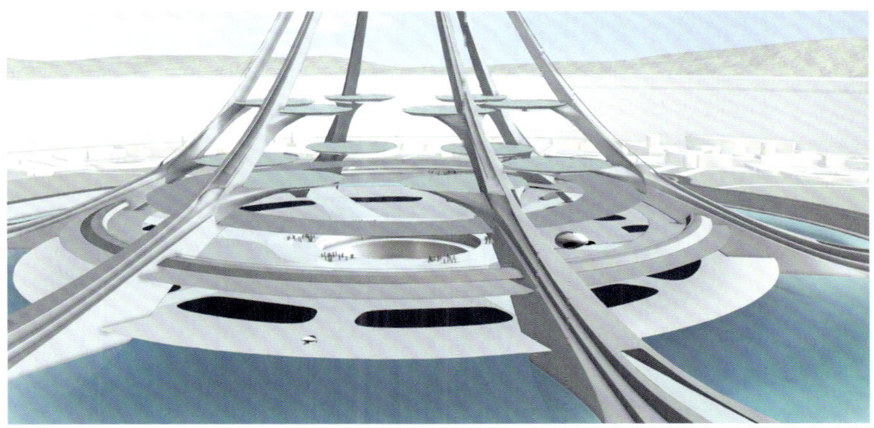

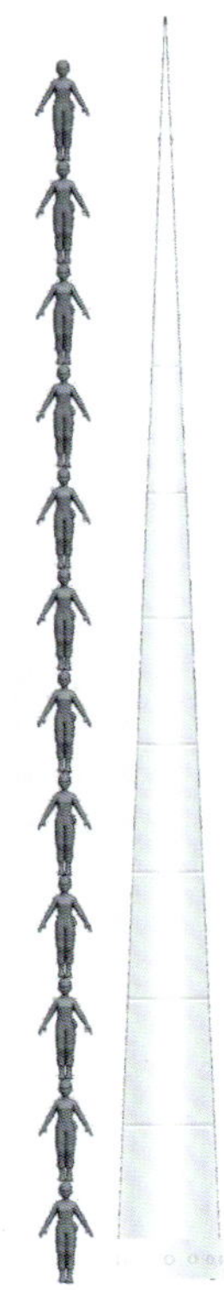

THIS PAGE
Artwork by
Marc Gabbana

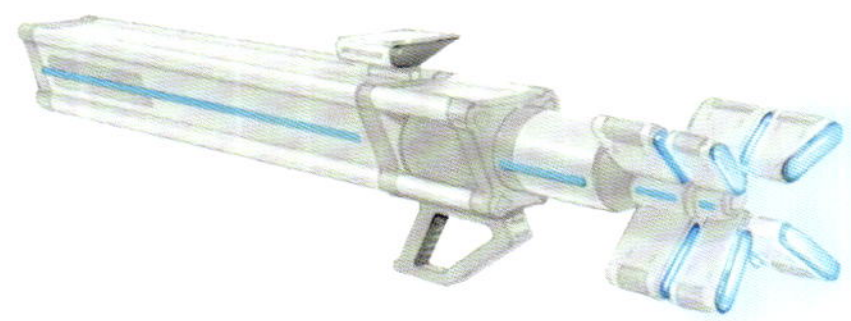

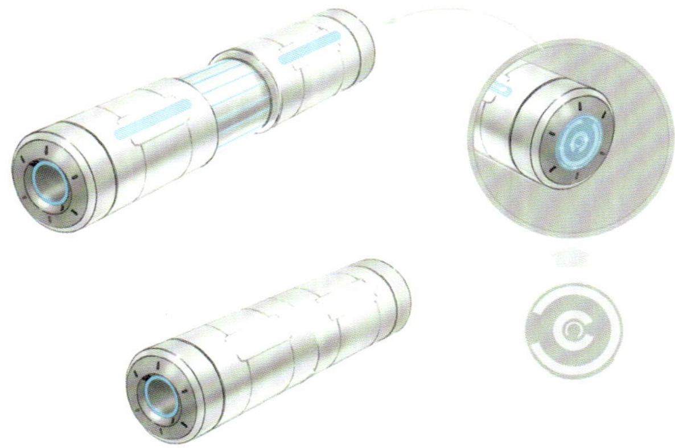

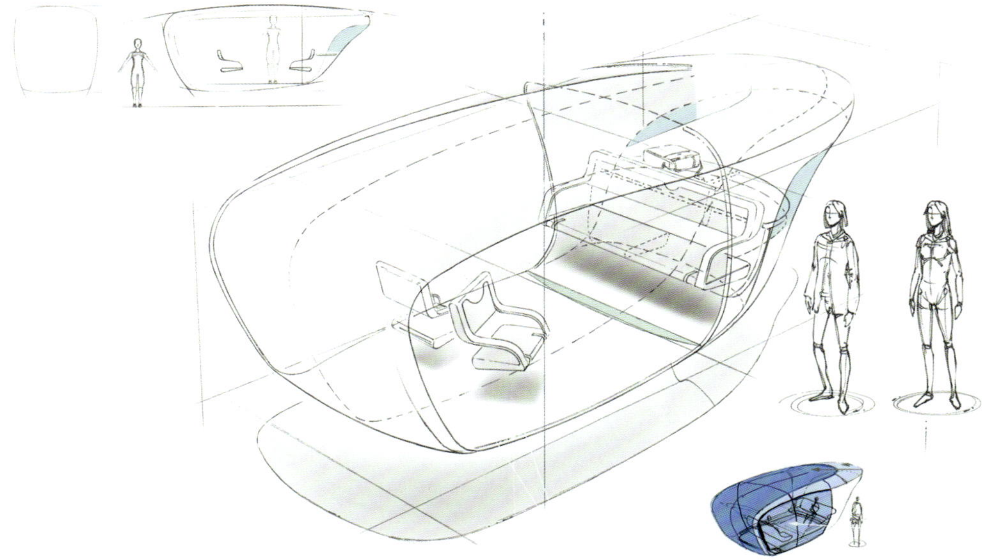

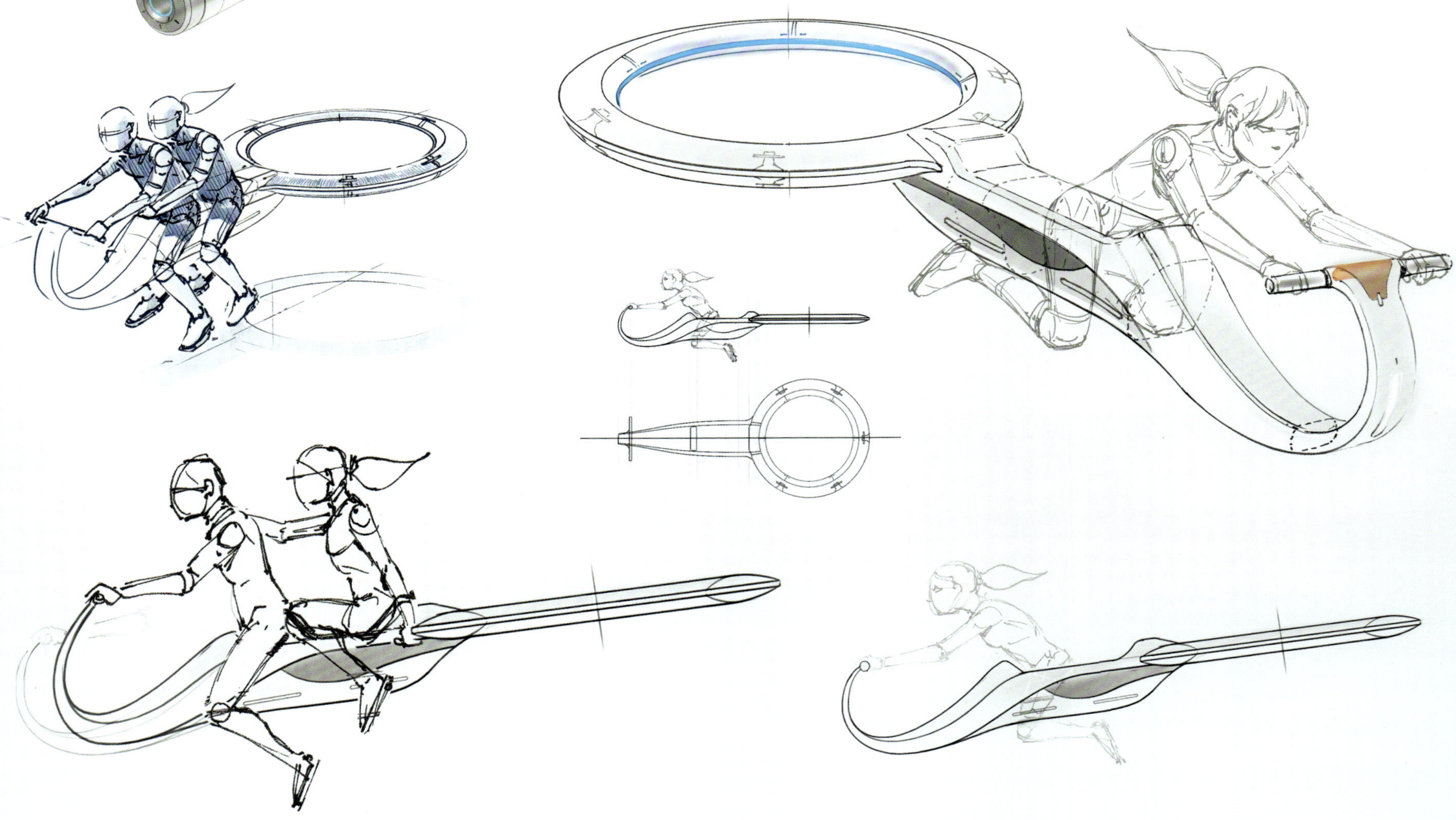

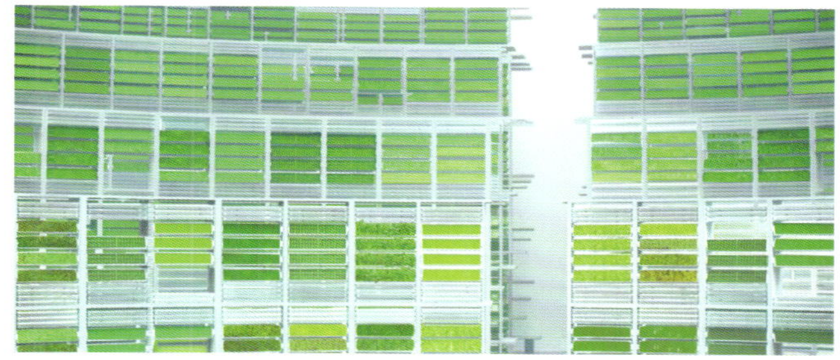

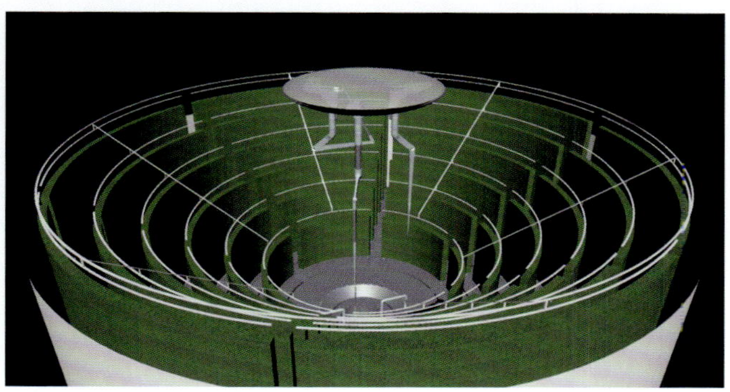

In the book, New Attica has a triangular pyramid shape, but in the series, the designers made sure everything had more of an arc or curve to it. Because the same company that made the bunkers made this world, the whole structure has a dome that projects the sky on it, just like Eva 9's sanctuary had projections in the bedroom and exercise room. "This is just like *The Truman Show*, where the main character had no idea that the sky wasn't really the sky until he got suspicious," says Harkness. "That's kind of the idea here too. People think they're above ground, but they are really under a concrete dome with things (like the weather and the time of day) projected on top of it. The whole thing is underground with a giant mesa that sits directly on top of it. The only way in and out of New Attica is if you fly out of a certain hidden wall in the mesa."

All the ships, the hoverbikes, and the gondolas that fly around New Attica were designed by Marc Gabbana. Functionality and necessity were the two governing design principles. "Our general thinking was 'design it the way you see it'. If there was something in the design that wasn't truly functional, we would get rid of it," says Harkness. "We didn't want to go backwards in the technology."

ABOVE & LEFT
Vertical farm by Nobertu Sasagawa and Marc Gabbana

BELOW
Concept art of crops

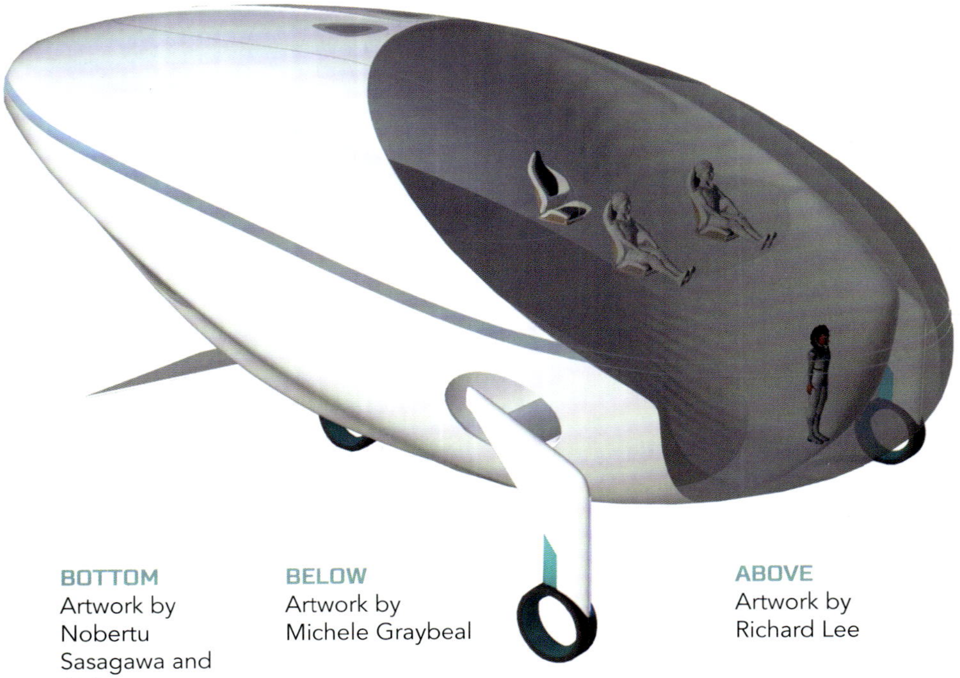

BOTTOM
Artwork by Nobertu Sasagawa and JJ Song

BELOW
Artwork by Michele Graybeal

ABOVE
Artwork by Richard Lee

RIGHT
Artwork by Michele Graybeal

FAR RIGHT
Hat and sunglasses by Kaitlyn Landry and Neysa Bove

RIGHT
New Attican models and costume design by Kalina Murat and Neysa Bove

BELOW
Men's shoes by Kaitlyn Landry and Neysa Bove

BOTTOM
Women's shoes by Kalina Murat and Neysa Bove

RIGHT
Artwork of Nova
by Neysa Bove

FAR RIGHT
Nova face study
by Chris Ables

BELOW
Nova and Gen
sketches by
Saira Vargas

ABOVE LEFT
Artwork of Gen
by Neysa Bove
and paint by
JJ Song

ABOVE
Artwork of Eva 9
by Neysa Bove

THIS PAGE
Costume artwork by Kalina Murat and Neysa Bove

BOTTOM LEFT
Shirt designs by Kaitlyn Landry and Neysa Bove

THIS PAGE
Costume artwork by Kalina Murat and Neysa Bove

CHARACTER

EVA 8 AND THE SANCBORNS

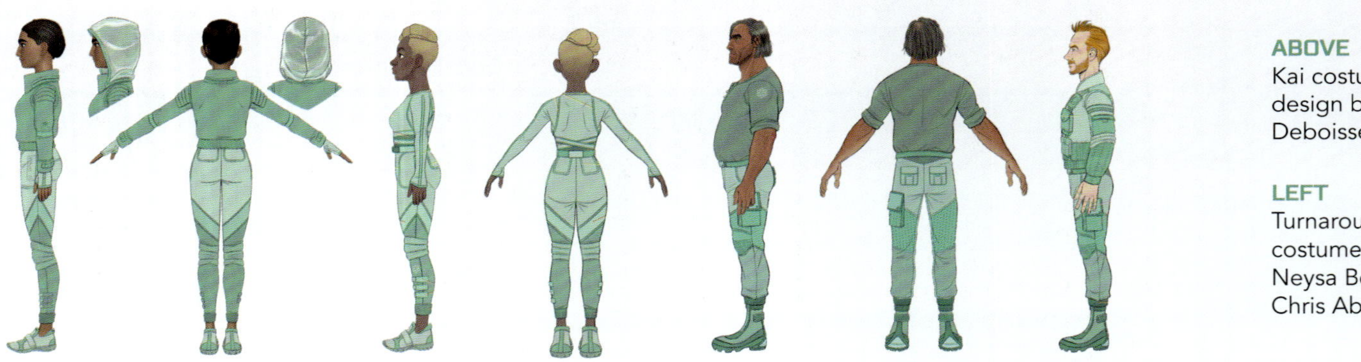

ABOVE
Eva 8 costume artwork by Ander Liza

ABOVE RIGHT
Violet and Xander costume design by Chris Ables

ABOVE
Kai costume design by Sylvain Deboissey

LEFT
Turnaround costumes by Neysa Bove and Chris Ables

RIGHT
Artwork of Olivier by Chris Ables

FAR RIGHT
Final still of Eva 8

TOP LEFT
Kai portrait by JJ Song

TOP CENTER
Xander portrait by Chris Ables

TOP
Violet portrait by Michele Graybeal

ABOVE
Eva 8 portrait by Michele Graybeal

ABOVE LEFT & CENTER
Margot and Frank portraits by Chris Ables and Michele Graybeal

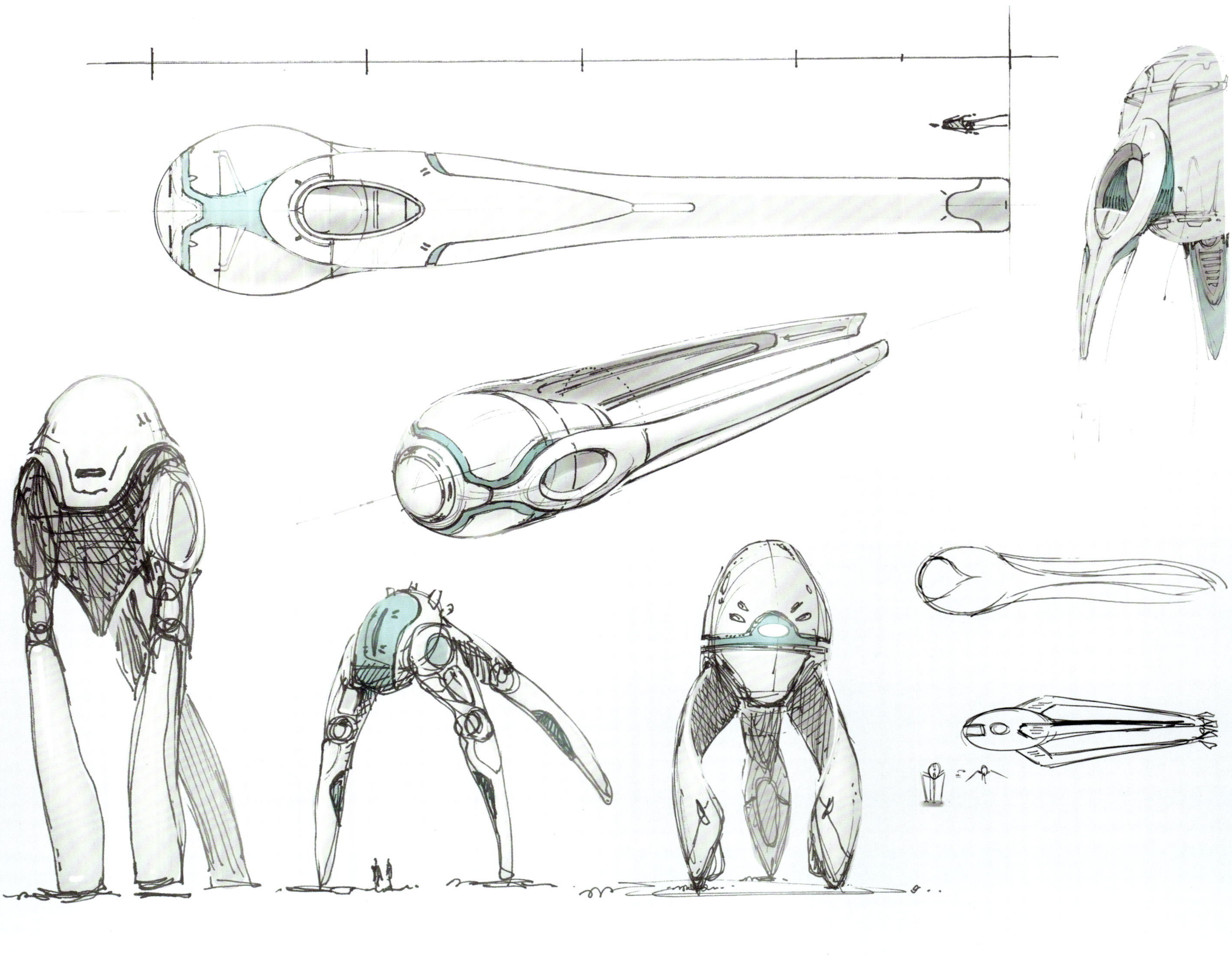

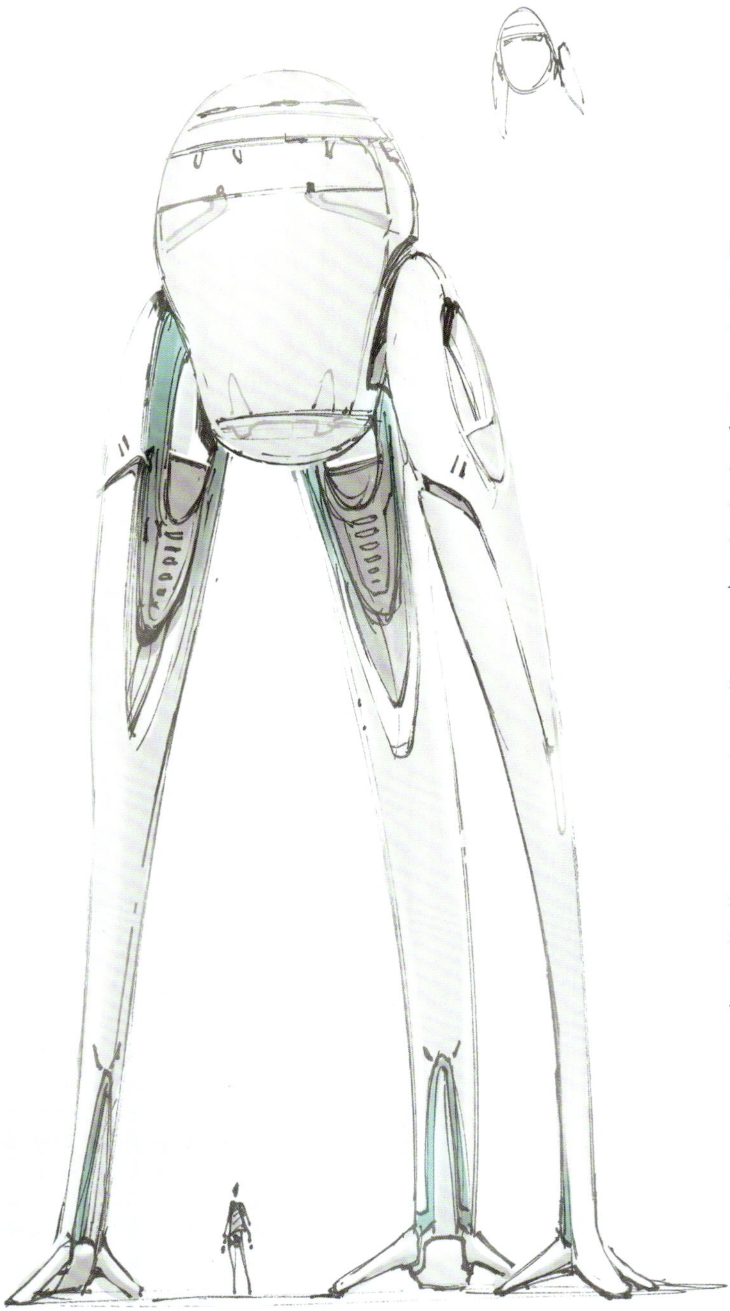

OBJECT

WARBOTS

DESIGNED BY CADMUS PRYDE AND MASS produced in New Attica, the warbots were created to exterminate all alien life on Orbona and help humans gain back control of the planet.

"We had a team of artists that tackled the design of all the technology used by the humans, led by artist Marc Gabbana," says Harkness. "The warbots went through many iterations. At first, they were a bit reminiscent of the machines in *War of the Worlds*. There is a high level of detail in their design, but we approached the task with the same perspective as all the other technological items in the series. If a design element is just extra or just for show, we took it out. Everything had to be functional. The warbots had to be multi-functional and handle almost any terrain. The top part needed to always stay balanced regardless of whether they're flying sideways or upside down."

Harkness points out that their weapons are not visible from the outside. "You can't see their guns as they are hidden underneath their 'skin'," he explains. "There's just a light energy source that begins to glow, and then these lasers shoot out. They have these arms that are almost fingerlike. They open like a tripod with a metallic tongue that has some texture on it and can grab things, which gives them a very octopus/squid-like physicality. The biggest warbot, which is the mothership, belongs to Cadmus, and you can see him riding around in it throughout the series."

THIS SPREAD
Artwork by
Marc Gabbana

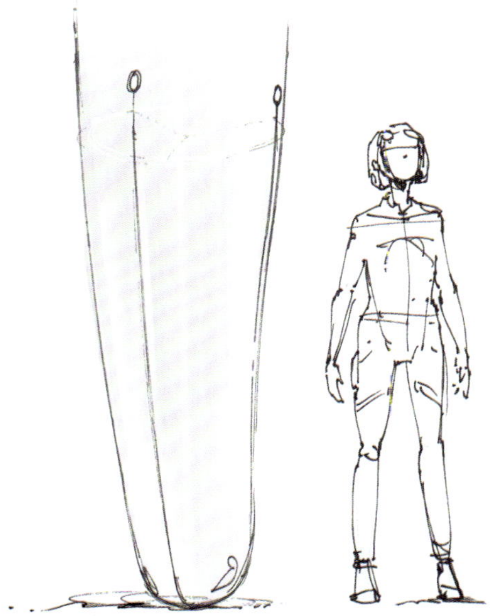

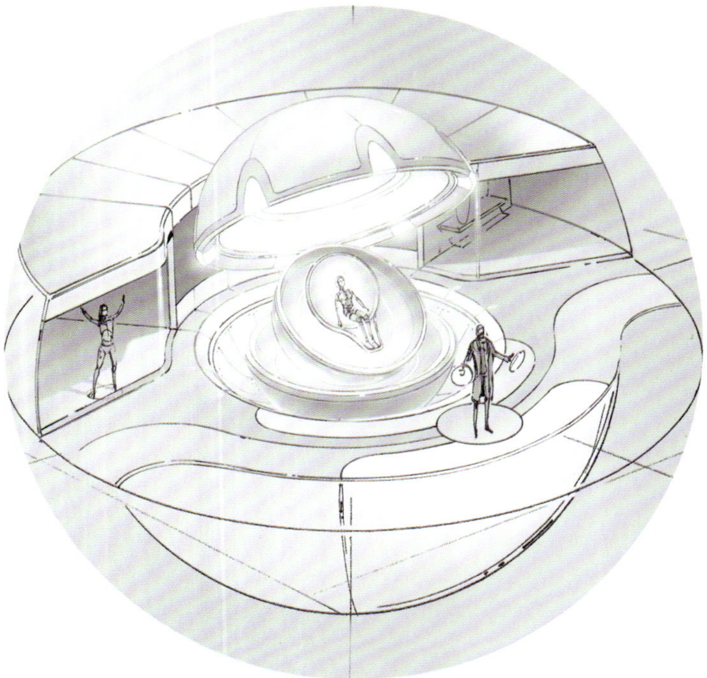

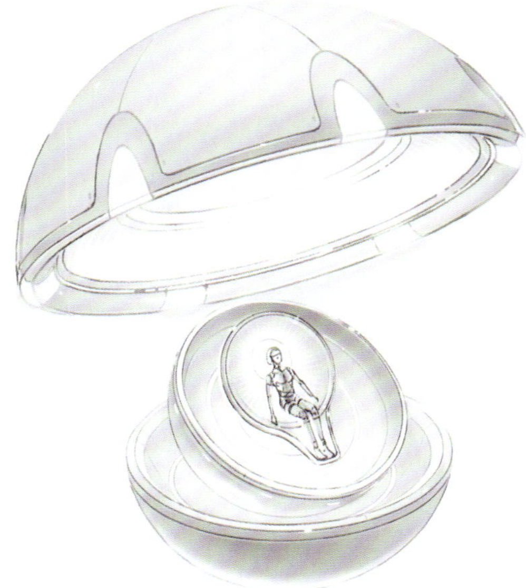

THIS PAGE
Artwork by
Marc Gabbana

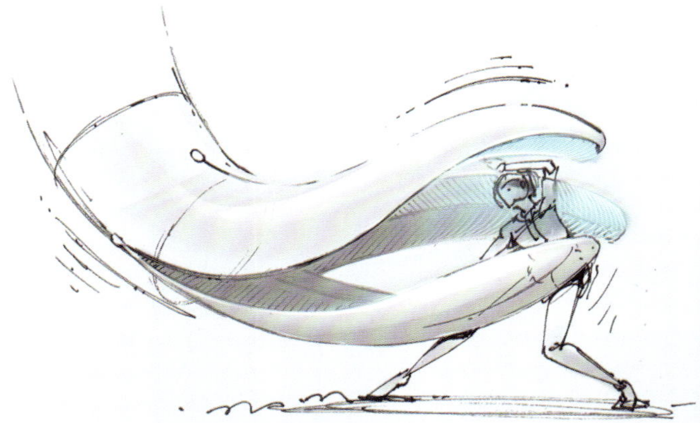

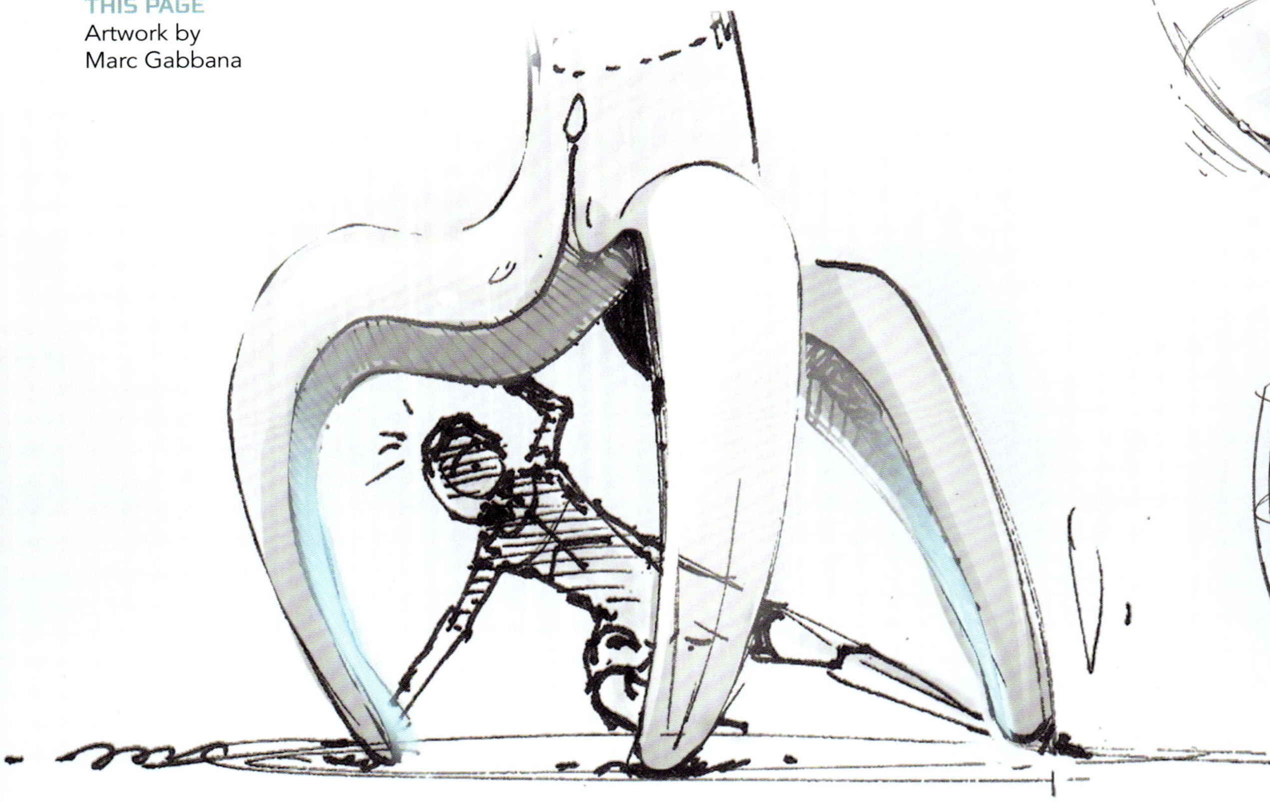

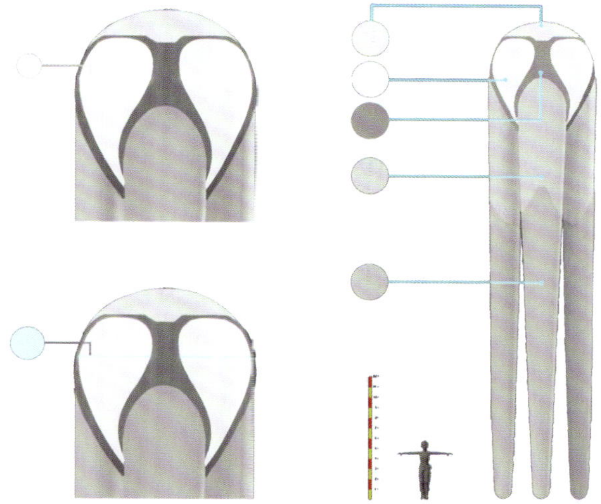

FAR LEFT
Artwork by
Richard Lee

LEFT
Artwork by
Richard Lee
and JJ Song

BELOW
Artwork by
Simon Baek

BELOW LEFT
Foot design by
Marc Gabbana

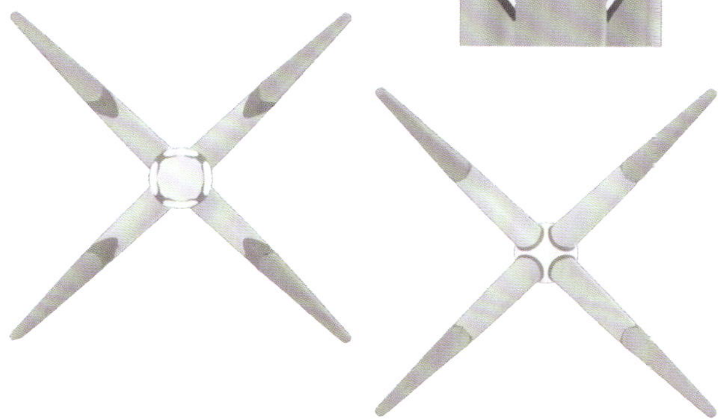

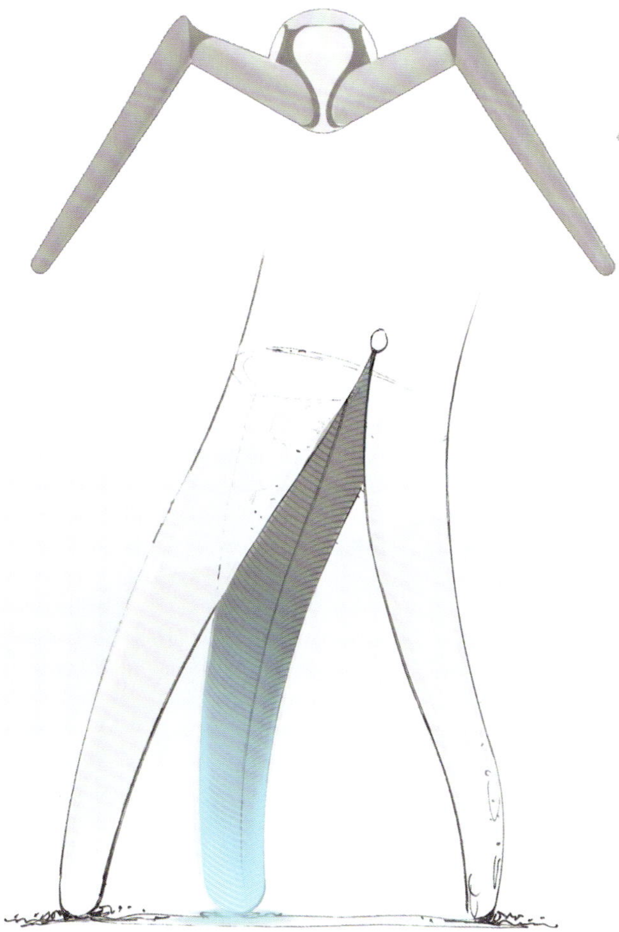

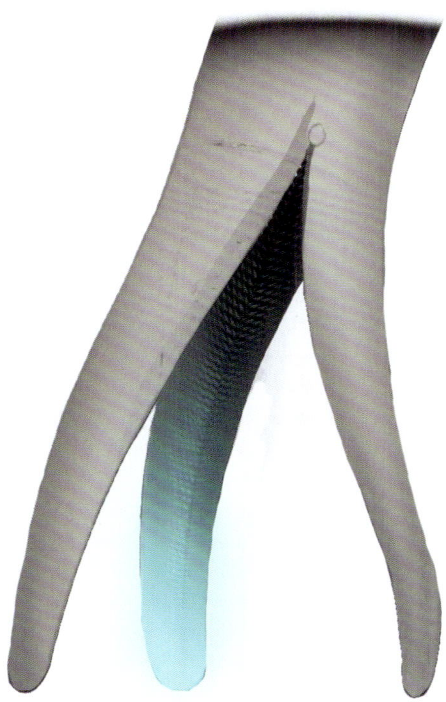

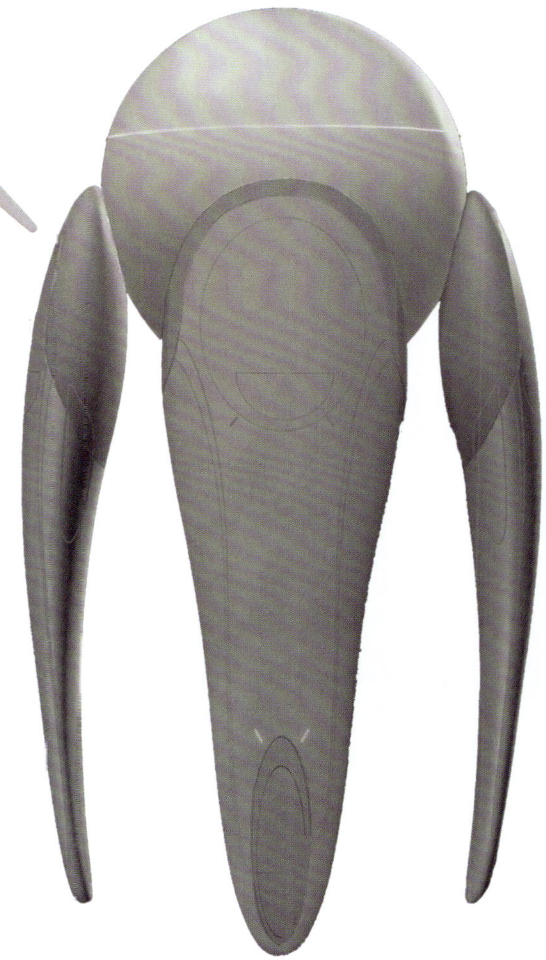

CREATURE

WANDERING FOREST

THIS PAGE
Artwork by
Michele Graybeal

OPPOSITE PAGE
Final still

THE WANDERING FOREST IS MADE UP OF A collection of alien wandering trees, which have tentacles that allow them to move to more suitable locations. They have a basic intelligence and are driven by migratory instincts. In the second season, we see these trees making their way to the heart of the forest, where they get recharged with their source of energy and continue their trips. With their woolly feet, they also act as ground sweepers. Arius lives in a hut nested on top of one of the wandering trees.

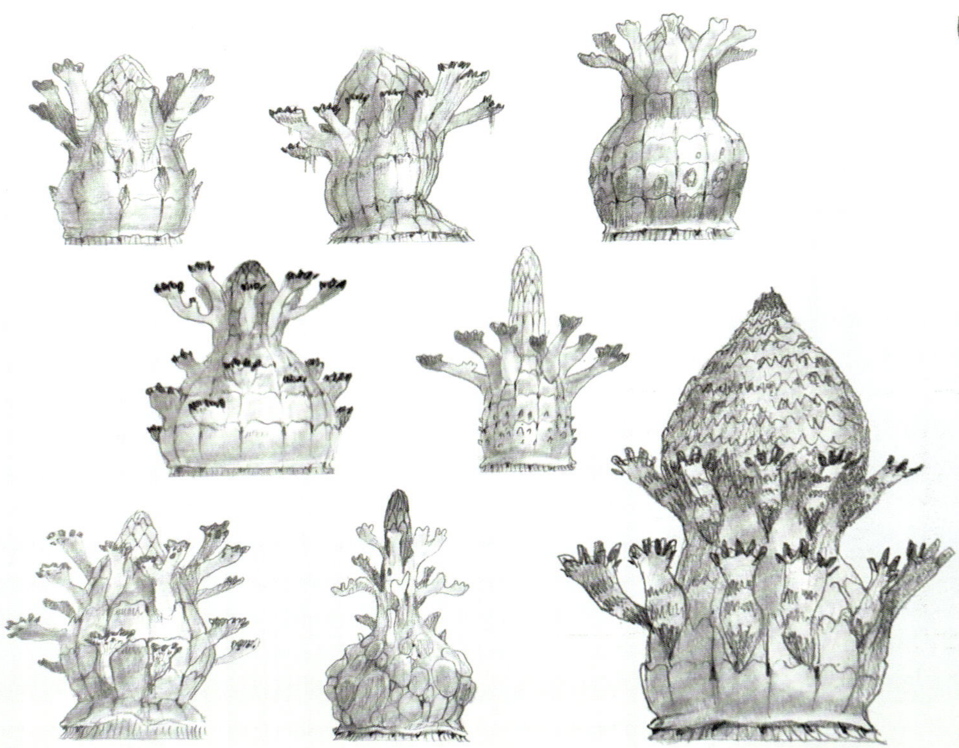

BELOW & RIGHT
Artwork by Armand Serrano

FAR RIGHT
Plant artwork by Julie Chon

BOTTOM
Whale outline and skeleton artwork by Armand Serrano and Martin Bergquist

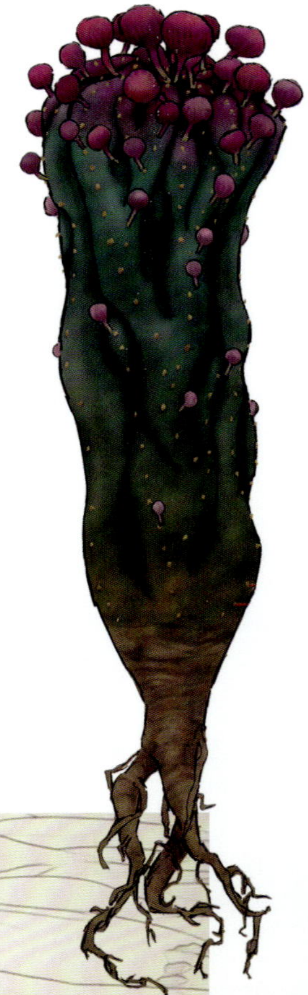

LOCATION

WASTELANDS

THE WASTELANDS OF ORBONA COULD BE Arizona or somewhere a little bit further east of that state in the US: imagine if the mesa was completely dry and extended for thousands of miles. Things have been decimated in this region since the moon came down. This region borders the Faunas village and its greener hunting grounds, and is home to creatures such as the giant moth-like Dawosu and the less terrifying, but also deadly, sandsnipers.

LEFT
Artwork by Nicolas Weis

BELOW
Artwork by Saira Vargas

THIS SPREAD
Artwork by
Armand Serrano
and Kalina Murat

CREATURE

DAWOSU

THIS PAGE Artwork by Saira Vargas

HAUNTINGLY BEAUTIFUL AND TERRIFYING AT THE same time, Dawosu is a giant moth-like creature with killer maternal instincts who comes face-to-face with Eva 9 in the second season of the show.

"I've been collecting butterflies and moths since I was a young boy, so I was very excited when I learned all about the Dawosu in our series," says Harkness. "One thing I've noticed is that butterflies and moths are almost never animated correctly in films and TV shows, so I was adamant that we got all the details right for this character in *WondLa*. Although it's a predatory creature, it has these colorful, patterned wings that almost put the observer in a bit of a trance. It has some massive teeth and a poisonous tail that kills its victims. However, at the end of the day, it is only trying to protect its eggs from other predators. That point is made clear when it connects with Eva 9, and the audience gets to understand that it's not a mindless killer."

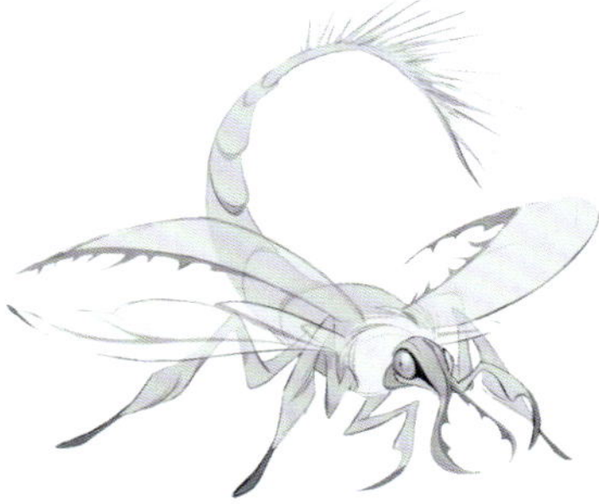

FAR LEFT
Artwork by Saira Vargas

LEFT
Artwork by Saira Vargas and Christine Kim

BELOW
Artwork by Michele Graybeal

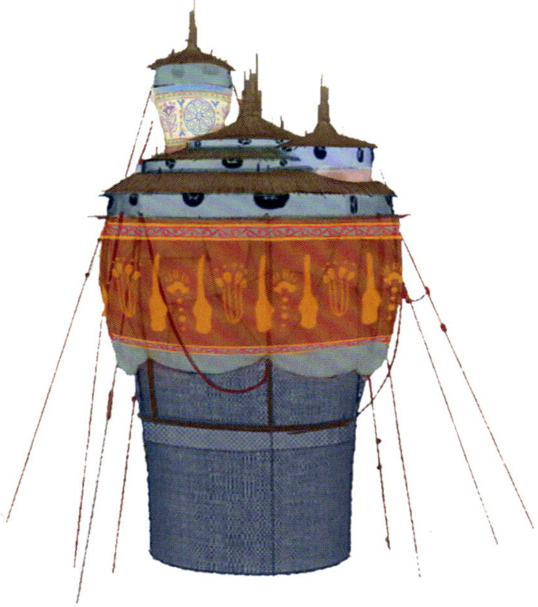

LOCATION

FAUNAS

THIS IDYLLIC CAERULEAN VILLAGE IS LOCATED east of New Attica. Led by Rovender's estranged father, Antiquus, Faunas stands out for its rustic charms and dependence on nature. Designed for the series by Armand Serrano (visual development artist on films such as *Zootopia*, *Ralph Breaks the Internet*, *Raya and the Last Dragon*, and the Marvel animated series *What If?*) this location explores the possible ways for a nomadic tribe to move their homes and families when encountering danger. Faunas sits on the edge of this expansive green field that is constantly growing out, and it is nestled among gigantic roots left over from the Tree of Life.

"Their whole village can go up pretty quickly because every building is held down by rope, and they're tethered to the ground like giant balloons," explains Harkness. "They can go off and land somewhere else."

THIS SPREAD
Artwork by Roy Santua and Kalina Murat

TEXTILE PATTERNS

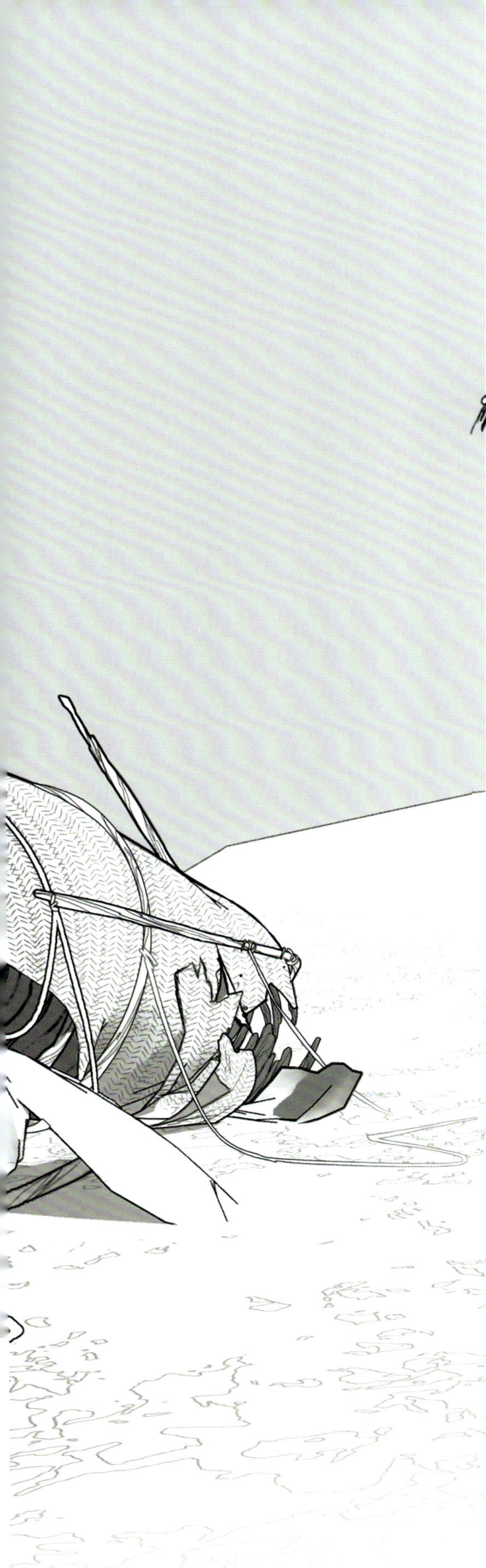

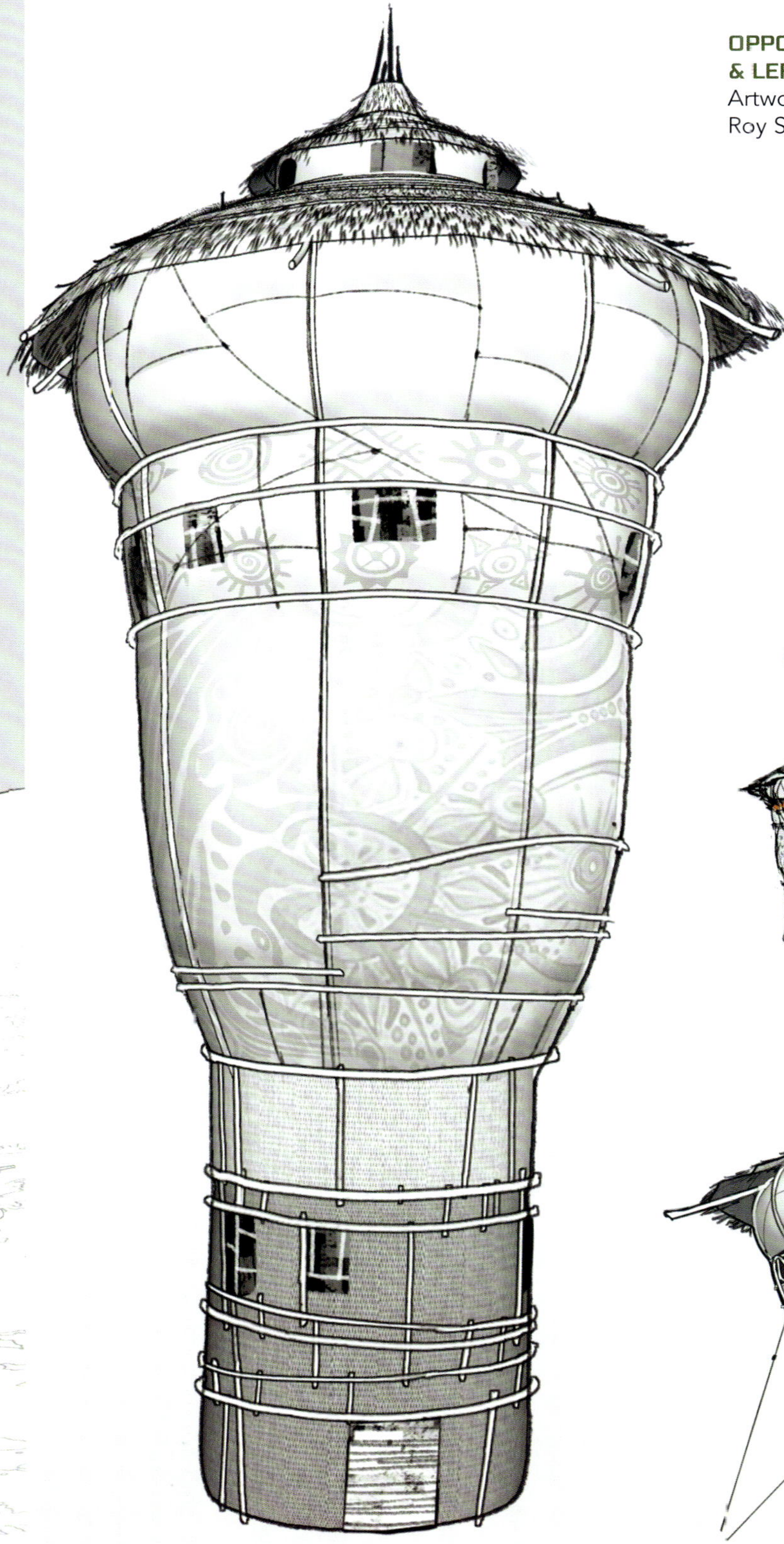

OPPOSITE PAGE & LEFT
Artwork by
Roy Santua

RIGHT
Pump by
Saira Vargas

BELOW
Color artwork by
Kalina Murat

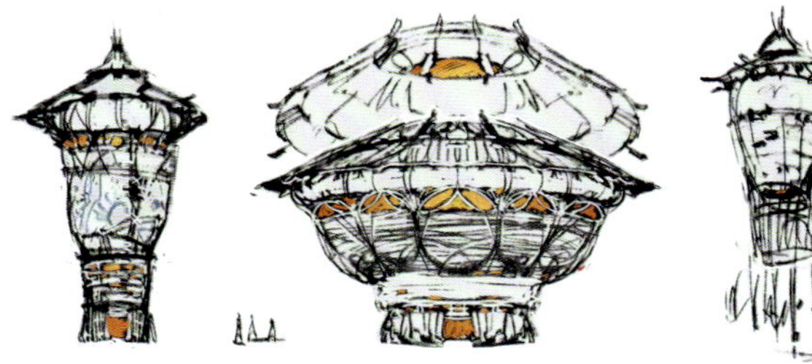

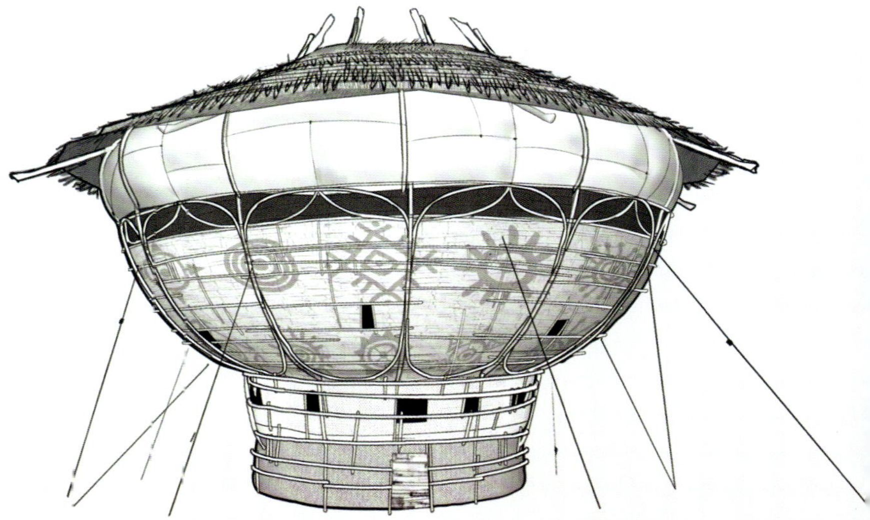

LEFT
Chimes and patterns by Neysa Bove

BELOW LEFT
Pot plant by Natalia Falciglia

RIGHT
Artwork by JJ Song

BELOW RIGHT
Artwork by Kalina Murat

BOTTOM
Artwork by Simon Baek

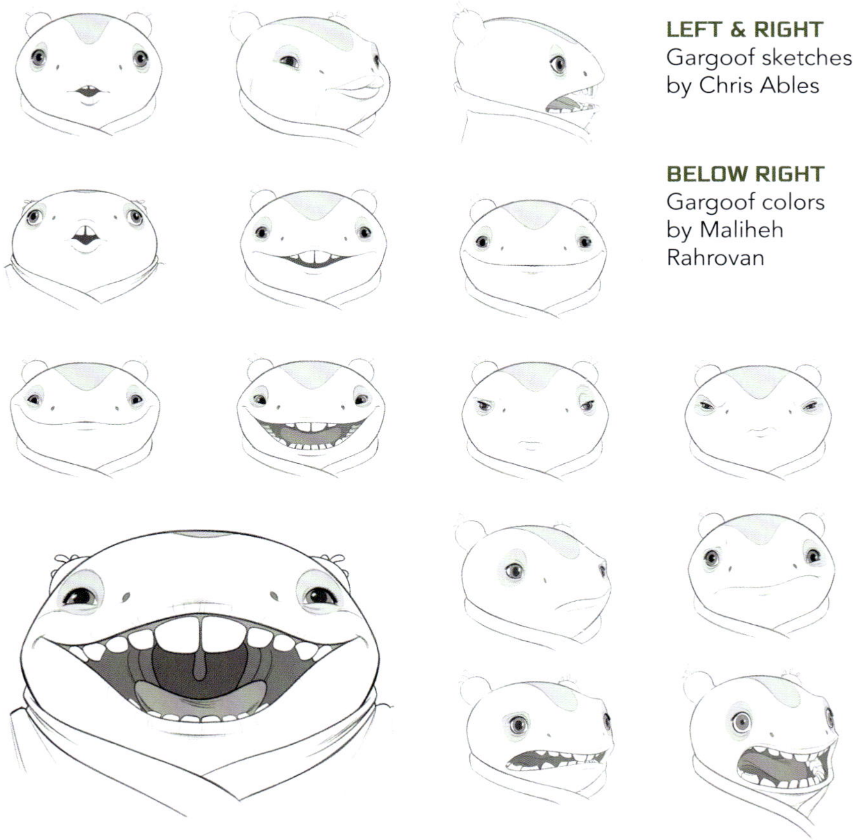

LEFT & RIGHT
Gargoof sketches by Chris Ables

BELOW RIGHT
Gargoof colors by Maliheh Rahrovan

RIGHT
Textile patterns by Neysa Bove and Kalina Murat

CREATURE

CAERULEANS

RIGHT
Artwork by Saira Vargas

BELOW
Textile patterns by Chris Ables

OPPOSITE PAGE
Artwork by Chris Ables

CAERULEANS ARE MEMBERS OF AN ALIEN RACE that came to Earth after the Great Migration. As a species, they are a peaceful, kind, and gentle people who are in harmony with the rhythms of nature around them. They shun technology and follow an agrarian-based lifestyle.

Like Rovender Kitt, who is 120 years old during the events of the series, they have very long life spans. Caeruleans's skin is blue and mottled, and their face reminds one of a catfish, turtle or a frog. Their knee joints bend backwards, and their feet have two giant toes and one small toe. Every year, they mark the arrival of new life on Orbona and the Heart of the Forest in a festive Bloom celebration with music, flowers, and paper lanterns.

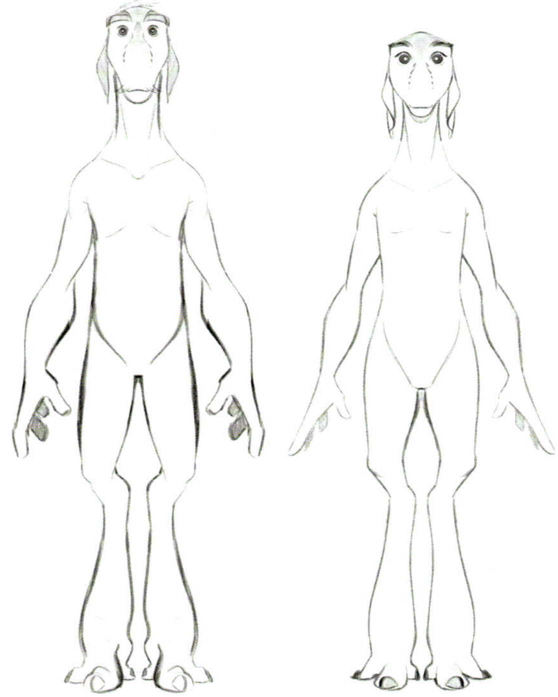

TEXTILE PATTERNS

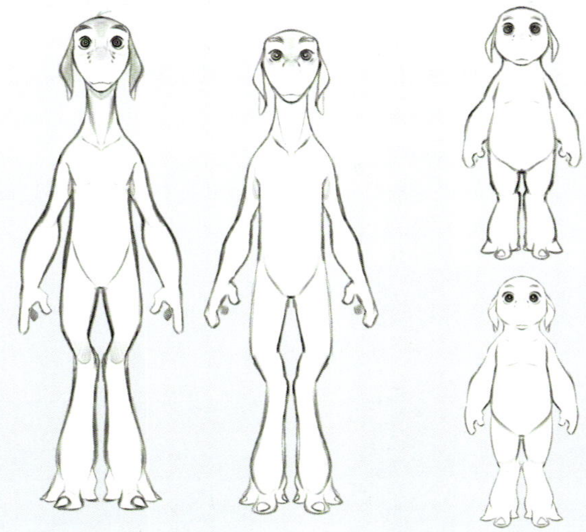

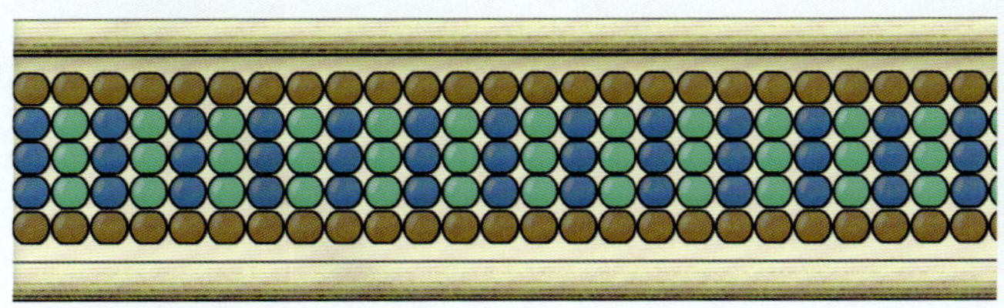

CHARACTER

ANTIQUUS

RIGHT
Costume by
Kalina Murat

BELOW
Staff by
Julie Chon

BELOW RIGHT
Portrait and
turnaround by
Michele Graybeal

ANTIQUUS IS ROVENDER KITT'S FATHER, THE ancient chief of the Caeruleans who, as a result of a misunderstanding, has banished his son from the tribe. The design of the character is very much in line with the original illustrations by Tony DiTerlizzi.

"Our character designer Sylvain Deboissy tapped into something wonderful with these characters," says Andy Harkness. "The Caeruleans are some of my favorite characters, not just Antiquus but all the elders in the tribe are just beautiful. They have these twisted braided hair and giant eyebrows that come down. Their defining feature is their color blue. Tony told us early on that the healthier and happier they are, the purer the blue is. The sadder and sicker they become, that blue turns to grey, and you can see that in Rovender. The elders have a steelier look to them, especially when you compare Antiquus to some of the young Caeruleans (such as Azura), you can really see the contrast in the colors."

CHARACTER

AZURA

TOP LEFT
Face study by
Chris Ables

LEFT
Artwork by
Chris Ables

BELOW
Conch shell
by Julie Chon

BOTTOM LEFT
Paint artwork by
Michele Graybeal

BOTTOM
Bead artwork
by Chris Ables

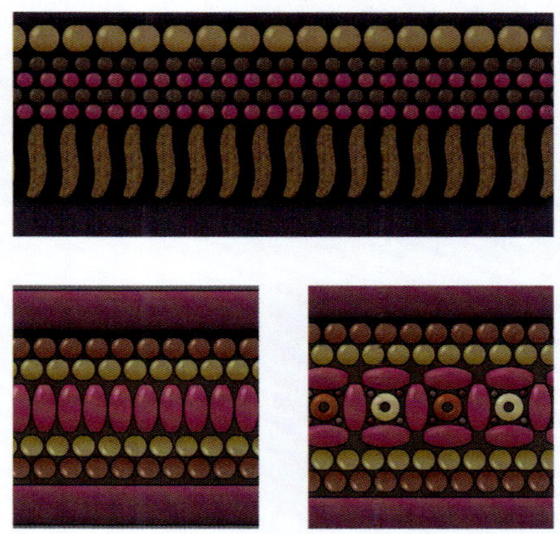

LOCATION

TAR PIT

THIS PAGE
Artwork by Martin Bergquist and Michele Graybeal

THE TAR PIT IS AN EXTREMELY DRY REGION THAT was probably once a pristine lake. It's located near Faunas, and was created after the moon was shattered into pieces and massive chunks of it landed on Earth, exposing subterranean tar and oil on the surface. "It's not somewhere you want to step in," says Andy Harkness. "In the third episode of the third season, you can see the remnants of a Lacus tree inside the Pit, but it's warped and distorted and the oil has killed most of it. It helps Eva 9 out, because at one point, the warbots are chasing Eva 9, and they get stuck in it."

CREATURE

TRUTH BIRD

INSPIRED BY TONY DITERLIZZI'S ORIGINAL illustrations for the book, the truth bird is a fantastic creature that is used in the Caeruleans' justice system and forces the accused or the witness to tell the truth. In the third season, Eva 9 seeks the bird out to save Rovender Kitt and help him get cleared from the crime of abandoning his family and tribe before the events of the show.

"The design was pulled from a variety of sources, from birds-of-paradise to rodents like hamsters, although it obviously has a beak," says Harkness. "The truth bird comes and goes in a magical, smoke-like manner. For the overall look, we also studied the refraction of light and the colors of the rainbow, as well as the iridescent texture of mother of pearls and insides of shells produced by molluscs. You can see the colors, but they are often hidden, and they appear and disappear."

LEFT
Artwork by
Ander Liza

ABOVE & BELOW
Sketches by
Saira Vargas

CREATURE

MUNT RUNNER

RIGHT
Artwork by
Michele Graybeal

BELOW
Sketches by
Saira Vargas

AMONG THE MANY UNUSUAL ALIEN ANIMALS roaming the plains of Faunas, munt runners are giant two-legged bird-like creatures that are used for transportation. "They're kind of like an ostrich or an emu on steroids," says Harkness. "They're very docile and cow or horse-like in nature. They have a huge beak, and their faces may remind you of hawks. They're probably about 15 to 20 feet tall and are usually seen with these beautifully designed saddles."

CHARACTER

REDIMUS

THE DORCEAN BROTHER OF BESTEEL IS imprisoned for most of the story by Queen Ojo. After making a bet with Besteel while the two were drunk, Redimus destroyed all the animals held at the Royal Menagerie. That's why Besteel had to catch and replace all the killed exhibits to free him from the prison. In the third season of the show, Redimus fights to save Eva 9 and the natural world.

THIS PAGE
Artwork by
Michele Graybeal

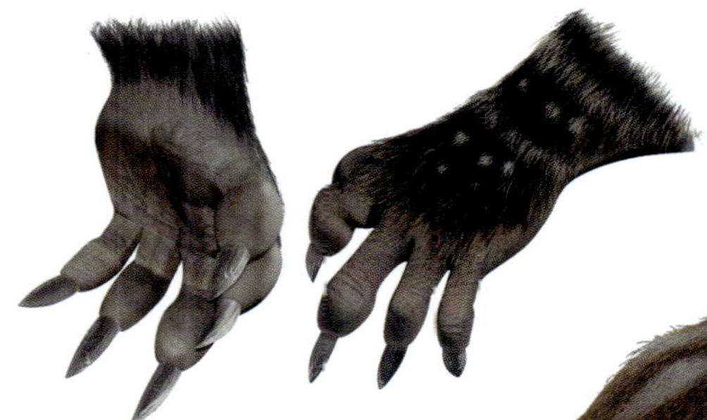

LOCATION

HEART OF THE FOREST

OPPOSITE PAGE
Artwork by Michele Graybeal and Kuba Kozlowski

RIGHT
Ball artwork by Nobuteru Sasagawa

BELOW
Final stills

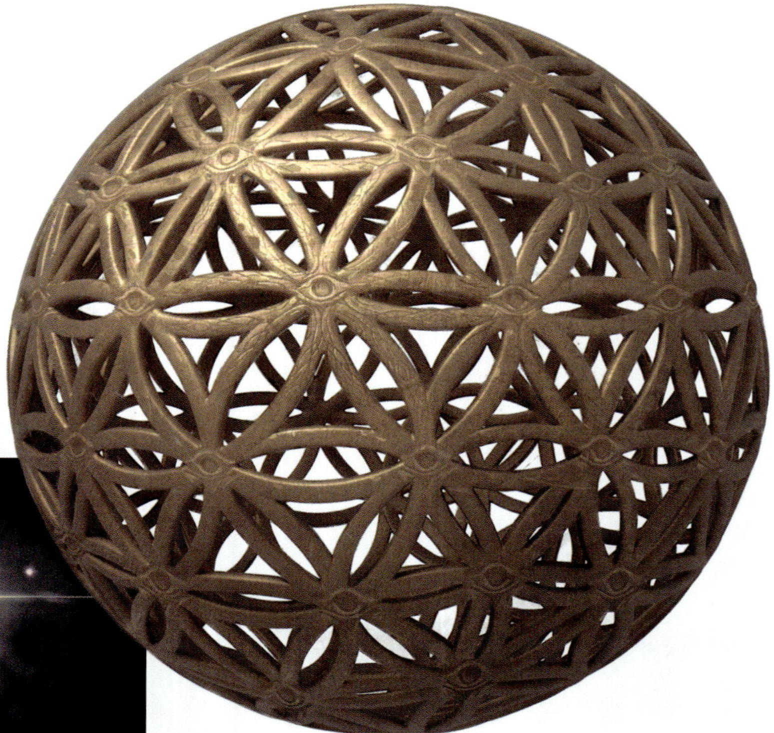

THIS PAGE
Artwork by
Michele Graybeal

OPPOSITE PAGE
Final still

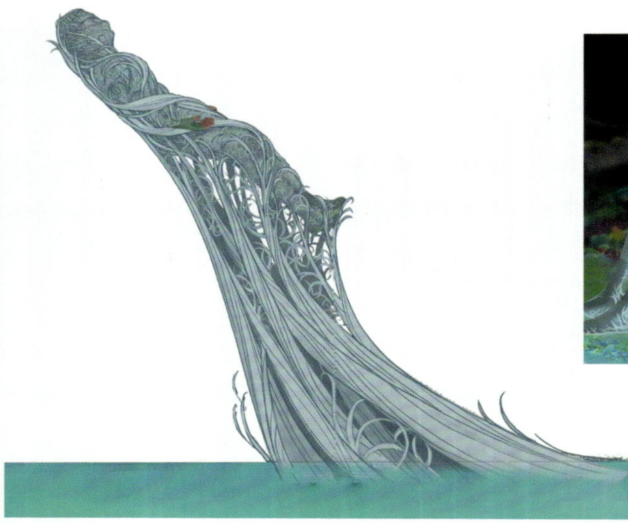

LOCATION

TREE OF LIFE

THIS PAGE
Artwork by
Michele Graybeal

TO CREATE THE THIRD SEASON'S PIVOTAL TREE of Life, the design team wanted to avoid similar iconic visuals that audiences have seen in major live-action and animated movies of recent years. "We definitely didn't want an *Avatar* tree," says Harkness. "We did a lot of research and went over all of them with John [Lasseter], so we knew exactly what not to do."

Harkness and his team looked at a wide variety of colorful flowers. "John wanted this to be the most beautiful thing in the world, so that when it comes to life and blooms, it really leaves a big impression. We studied violets and lilies, although we were looking for this huge tree. We needed to bring a hyper amount of detail at the bottom of the tree as the roots go out and they form a mandala pattern. That pattern is repeated a lot, and we see it spreading everywhere. The seed erupts and giant vines begin to grow all over the place."

Lasseter asked Harkness to create a painting showing Orbona in all its glory. "That was one of the last things I did on the show," he recalls. "It was only for a matte painting—basically one shot that I did in VR, as the camera lifts wide, and we see this world being restored to its purest colors imaginable, with clean air all around. It was the perfect way to end this incredible project. We really left it all on the field. I'm so proud of this crew who jelled so well because we all wanted *WondLa* to be something great and a place we'd want everyone to visit again and again."

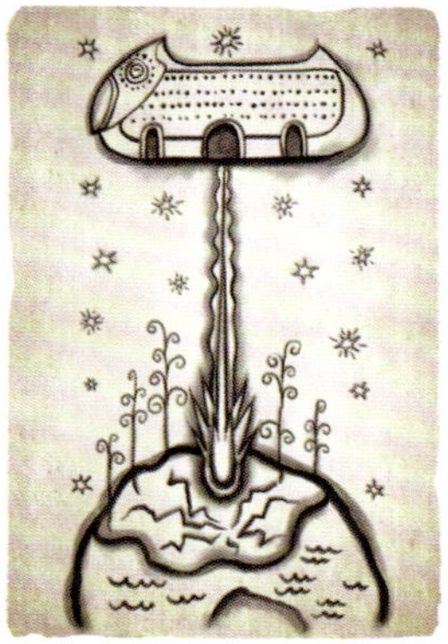

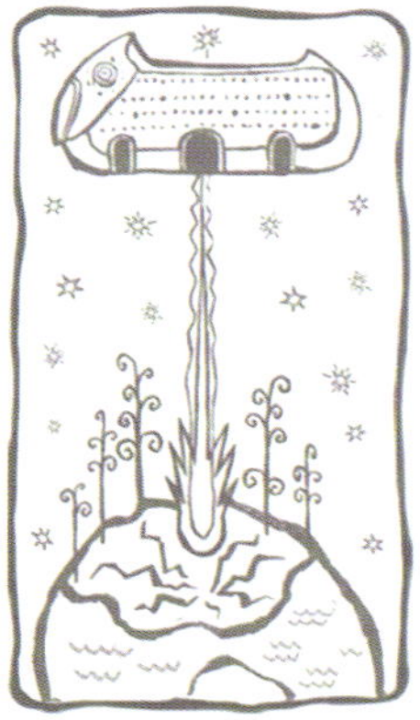

OBJECT

TAPESTRIES

WE FIRST SEE THE INTRICATELY WOVEN tapestries in the home of Darius, the ancient Ars an oracle that tells Eva 9 about the faith of the humans early in the first season of *WondLa*. These tapestries offer a visual representation of both the past and the future of life on the planet.

TOP LEFT
Artwork by Julie Chon and paint by JJ Song

BELOW
Artwork by Roy Santua and Julie Chon

CHARACTER

ARIUS

LEFT & BELOW
Chimes and stones by Simon Baek

BOTTOM
Artwork by Kalina Murat

THIS PAGE
Artwork by
Simon Baek

MAKING MUSIC FOR AN OTHERWORLDLY UNIVERSE

HARMONIC CONVERGENCE

OPPOSITE PAGE Artwork by Roy Santua and Julie Chon

JOY NGIAW'S ETHEREAL MUSIC FOR *WondLa* plays as important a part as any of the major players in this memorable series. Using a wide range of global influences and instruments, the talented composer colors the show with evocative harmonies and unique sounds.

"I remember the first thing our director, Andrew Schmidt, told me was that he wanted the main theme to be both epic and intimate," Ngiaw recalls. "These are two big contrasting ideas, because the *WondLa* theme must be able to be huge and adventurous, but you also need to scale it down to convey those intimate and emotional moments. I spent a lot of time coming up with the right notes. We hear this theme every time the show's main title comes up, so I was really pleased that we were able to go as huge as possible, while also being able to make it super intimate in places."

The talented composer, who also created the music for Skydance's acclaimed 2021 short *Blush* (directed by Joe Mateo), says she was fortunate that she came on board early in the series' development process. "We had many months to really nail all the details down, including the show's many locations, themes, and the kind of instruments we could use to create various characteristics we needed," says Ngiaw. "We started out with the main theme, which also represents Eva 9, and then we fleshed out the ones for the other characters such as MUTHR, Besteel, and Rovender, before moving on to the locations."

Looking back at the experience, she says she really loved the way she was encouraged to explore different sounds and instruments from countries all around the world to come up with the various characters and realms of *WondLa*. "The filmmakers would discuss the specific traits of each location, for example Lacus is a very community-centric place so perhaps I could use African or Amazonian percussion instruments, in contrast with Solas which is a very artificial kingdom," Ngiaw recalls. "So, it was very helpful that I was allowed to sit in on meetings and understand more about different aspects of the show. It was a great canvas and musical playground for me."

The process of creating each theme began with Ngiaw coming up with the bare-bone melody on the piano or just humming the music. "I did all the vocals myself, and I also added some unusual elements like recording the sound of a Slinky toy and creating a percussion sound out of it," she notes. "I layered some weird sound design elements on top of a Chinese erhu. I was able to experiment with various southeast Asian plucked instruments like the Korean gayageum and Chinese guzheng. We even added music from a Mongolian choir, so everything was at our fingertips to create the perfect sound for each world."

Ngiaw says she discovered many new sounds and instruments as she researched the project. "I was playing with some African instruments at a local music store, and came across a balafon, which is a gourd-resonated xylophone used to communicate with birds in the rainforest," she shares. "It was so wonderful to find these non-Western instruments which I could program into my scores. I felt very fortunate that the filmmakers trusted my musical instincts and allowed me to experiment with so many different sounds throughout the 20 episodes. From creating the music for diverse alien tribes, to composing the themes for all these wonderful characters, *WondLa* was the very definition of an epic, dream project!"

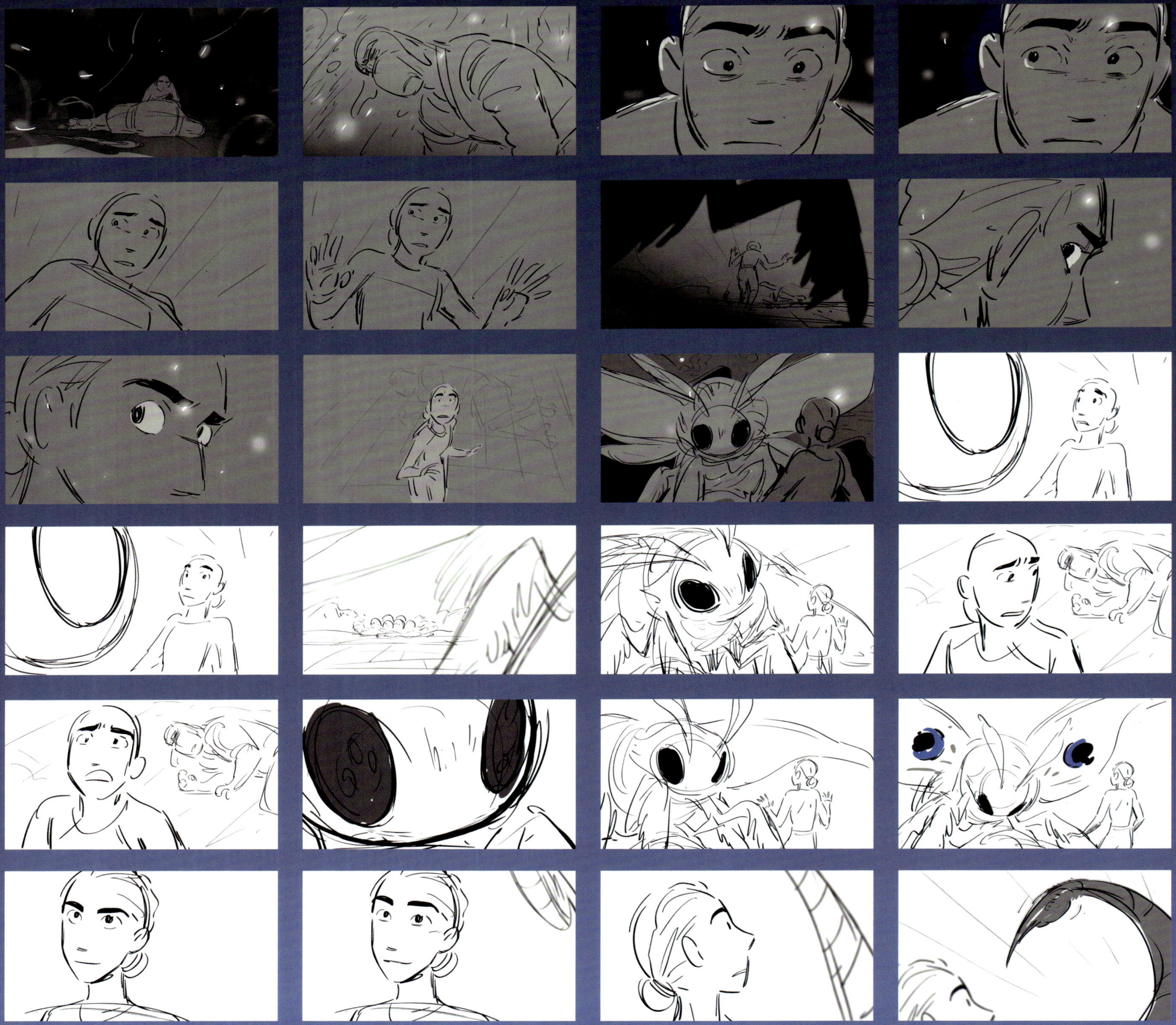

ANATOMY OF A SCENE

EVA 8'S WARNING

EVA 9 COMES FACES TO FACE WITH one of the giant, moth-like Dawosus in one of the most suspenseful and pivotal episodes of the second season. The enigmatic nature of this creature opens our heroine's eyes to the complex moral nuances of the world.

"There are moments on every picture where the best and most important ideas are going to need extra time to figure out," says Cosanella. "We didn't settle in our storytelling and made sure every frame had a purpose. This required a great deal of iteration and creative scheduling along the way—we found opportunities where we could open the schedule and support the creative needs. This beat in the story required us to enlist more help from our creative leaders."

Our goal was to create a clear relationship between Eva 8, Eva 9, and the environment," he adds. "We needed tension, and this sequence allowed for that opportunity. Eva 9 was to be an active participant across the series; however, she couldn't always be right. This sequence showed that vulnerability, while also building the sisterly relationship."

Schmidt says the reason the sequence stands out is because it's the point in the story when Eva 9 and Eva 8's clashing world views come to head. "Eva 9 believes that she understands and can communicate and reason with all things Orbonian. Eva 8, on the other hand, believes that Orbona is a world full of danger and things that can kill you. As the scene plays out, in this particular moment, Eva 8 is proven right and Eva 9 is proven wrong as the Dawosu attacks and Eva 8 is forced to protect her sister."

The key to the success of the scene was to make sure the audience stayed in Eva 9's perspective. "We purposefully hid the reveal of the Dawosu from the audience up until Eva 9 sees it for the first time, so that the audience could experience it with her," says Schmidt. "When we revealed the Dawosu, we played it as a magical moment, a majestic, beautiful creature... up until the very moment when it turns on Eva 9. Then the audience experiences that change in tone, the emotion of 'Uh-oh, I think I made a mistake,' along with Eva 9."

Creative director Grace Davis believes this scene is one of the most critical scenes over the entirety of the series. "It's the literal midpoint of our entire show. Eva 9 is fleeing this unknown force that Eva 8 is terrified of. She has told her that there's something that attacks from the sky. Eva 9, along with the audience, believes that whatever it is she can reason with it. We've seen up to this point that Eva 9's greatest power is her ability to communicate, so she believes that whatever this force is, she will be able to reach it."

Harkness explains that the scene explores how misunderstandings can make things quickly deteriorate when fear is involved. "When Eva 9 asks the Dawosu not to hurt them, the creature suddenly softens, revealing it is only protecting its family, just as Eva 9 is protecting Rovender," he explains. "They have a moment of mutual empathy that is short-lived when the creature's instincts to feed take over. Eva 9 is

OPPOSITE PAGE
Storyboards

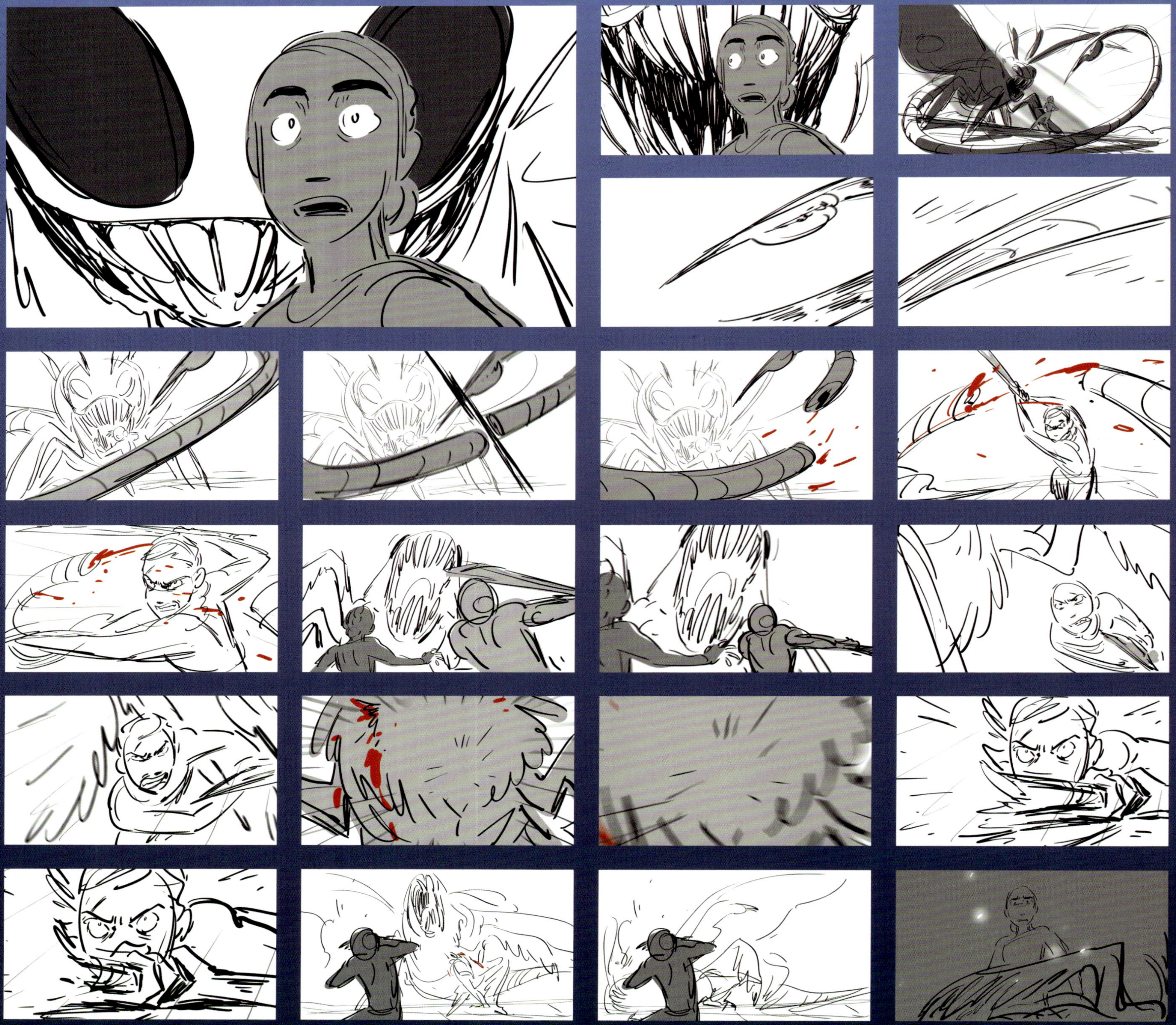

threatened, and the Dawosu is killed. It's a sad moment because they were so close to connecting, but it's still a vision of what could be."

Harkness points out that the scene takes place at night, which helped the team create an atmosphere of shadow, silhouette, and mystery. "However, there is enough light to see the softening of the creature's face and its expression," he adds. "Overall, the scene is cast in blue, which brings all the colors together to focus on the acting and heighten the emotion. The rest of the world falls off into shadow creating a theatrical feeling that adds to the drama of the moment. I am a butterfly and moth nerd, so for me, getting the correct lighting on the wings was important. Also, the wings are soft and semi-translucent, so we can see the moonlight burn through them a little."

For Herrig, it was quite critical to make the Dawosu feel believably cuddly and friendly, and then ease into it being a villain with the most fantastic teeth the team could hope for. "Walking the line of suspense and horror while making the look generally beautiful and appropriate for *WondLa* was quite the challenge. The shots where we reveal the teeth of the Dawosu with a rack focus (changing focus during a continual shot) were very successful across all departments. The look of this horrific character married with the moon-lit lighting design and this offered a slightly eerie sequence that really supported the emotions of the story."

"Eva 9's powers are put to the greatest possible strain during this encounter," concludes Davis. "It's when our underdog values of connection, coexistence and understanding meet with the dominant values which defend this 'us versus them' point of view. Eva 8 says, 'There are just some things that cannot be reasoned with,' and Eva 9 realizes that her powers and values have failed her. It's a reckoning that both we as the audience and Eva 9 never see coming."

THIS SPREAD
Storyboards

COLOR KEY

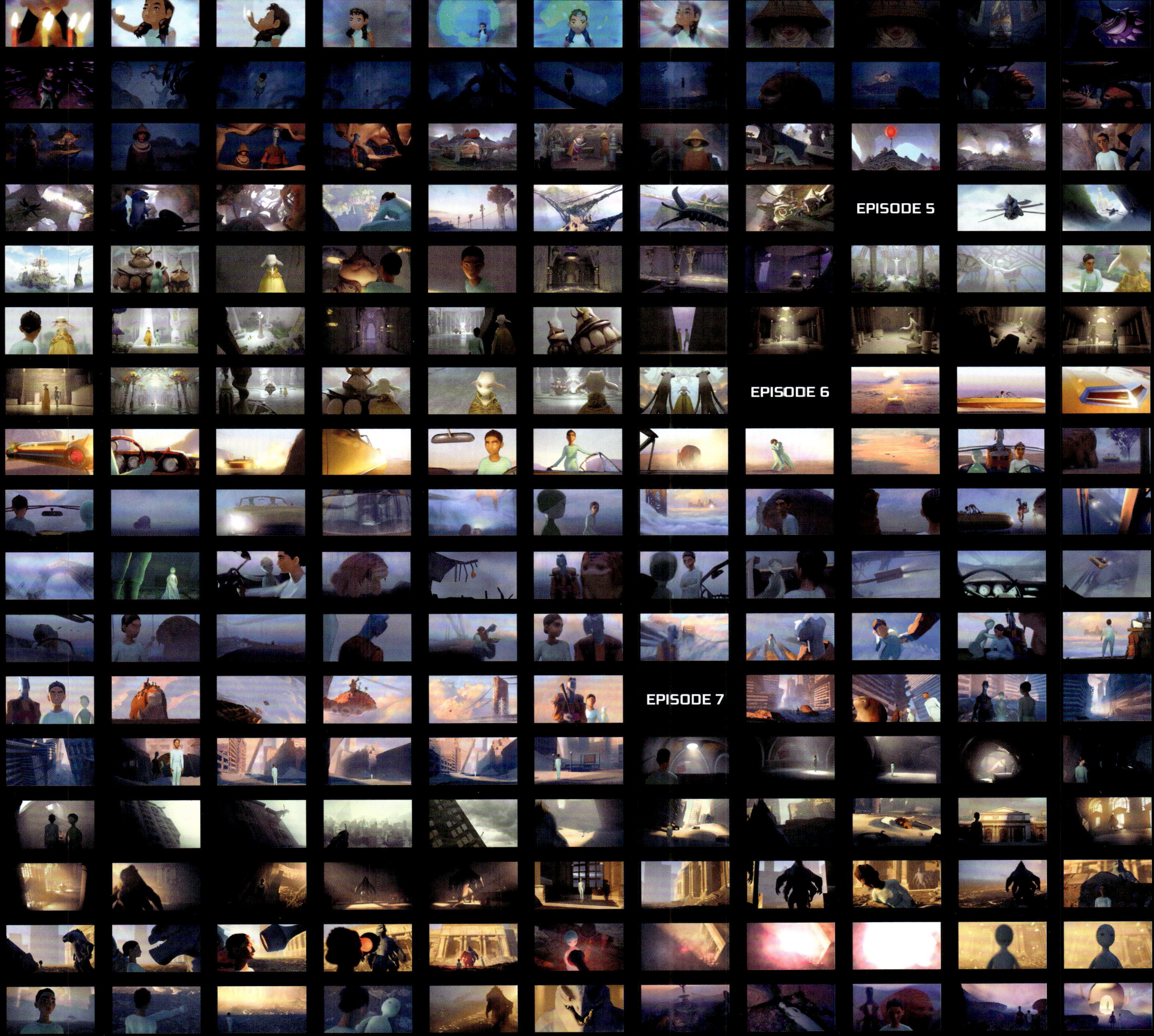
EPISODE 5
EPISODE 6
EPISODE 7

ACKNOWLEDGMENTS

I WOULD LIKE TO THANK ALL THE TALENTED AND brilliant artists and creative folks at Skydance Animation for sharing their journey to *WondLa* with me and who generously offered their insights and memories of making three seasons of this acclaimed series.

I am so grateful to each and every one of you—Torbin Bullock, Neysa Bove, Tony Cosanella, Tony DiTerlizzi, Bobs Gannaway, Andy Harkness, Josh Herrig, John Lasseter, Richard Lee, Joy Ngiaw, Maliheh Rahrovan, and Yuri Senoo. A special thanks to the wonderful Helen Rodas Escobar who always brings sunshine and magic to each and every interaction, Titan Books' amazing designer Kerry Lewis, and our fantastic editor Frankie Piscitelli who shepherded this project like a true superhero.

The book is dedicated to my terrier sidekick, Gizmo the wonder dog, who thinks the whole book should have been about Otto!

BOTTOM LEFT Meego by Simon Baek